Life in the UK Test
Practice
Questions

Questions and answers for the British citizenship test

Published by Red Squirrel Publishing

Red Squirrel Publishing
Suite 235, 15 Ingestre Place, London W1F 0DU United Kingdom

www.redsquirrelbooks.com

First edition published in 2006
Tenth edition – First impression

ISBN: 978-1-907389-70-2

Edited by Henry Dillon and Alastair Smith

Proofreading by Nomtha Gray

Typeset by Antony Gray

Printed and bound in the UK by Micropress

CONTENTS

This book is dedicated to the memory of our wonderful friend and colleague Martin Cox, who worked tirelessly on the design and typesetting of these guides for 12 years.

INTRODUCTION

Choosing to become a British citizen is an exciting decision, one made by thousands of people each year. However, the decision to become a British citizen or permanent resident is only the start of what can be a long and challenging journey. The application process is complex, time-consuming and expensive.

Home Office statistics show that around three in ten people failed the test in 2014. At £50 for every test taken this is an expensive mistake, and an unnecessary one. Feedback from our customers shows that 94% pass first time.

Tens of thousands of people take the Life in the UK Test every year, but not all of them pass. However, with the right preparation, you can be one of those who passes **first time**.

About this book

This book is designed to test your knowledge and understanding of the official study materials. This introduction offers advice on how to prepare for the test and guidance on the kinds of question you will face.

There are 20 complete practice tests, each containing 24 questions in the same format as the actual test. The questions are all based on the testable sections of the official study materials, and these are the following chapters:

- The values and principles of the UK
- What is the UK?
- A long and illustrious history
- A modern, thriving society
- The UK government, the law and your role.

Take some time to read through the following sections carefully. They tell you about all the features of this book and will enable you to get as much out of it as possible.

Page references

The answer tables for each practice test include a page reference to the 2020 study materials. They refer to our books, *Life in the UK Test: Handbook 2020* (ISBN: 978-1-907389-71-9), *Life in the UK Test: Study Guide 2020* (ISBN: 978-1-907389-68-9) and *Life in the UK Test: Study Guide & CD ROM 2020* (ISBN: 978-1-907389-69-6).

These page references tell you exactly which bit of the official study materials each question is based on. You can use these to revise difficult topics and target your study.

How to prepare for the test

1. Study the materials

The first and most important step of your preparations is to study the complete official study materials. These are found in the Home Office handbook, *Life in the United Kingdom: A guide for new residents* and are reproduced in our titles, *Life in the UK Test: Study Guide* and *Handbook*. You can find more information about these books at **www.lifeintheuk.net/books**

It is essential that you read and understand the testable chapters before taking your test. Taking practice tests alone will not prepare you for the real test.

2. Take practice tests

Once you've finished thoroughly reviewing the study materials, you should check if you are ready to take the test by completing the practice tests from this book.

When you sit your official test, you will be given 45 minutes to complete the test. So when you take a practice test, you should allow yourself the same time. The pass mark in the official test is at least 75% – or only six incorrect answers. Again, this is what you should aim to score when you take a practice test.

If you can consistently score at least 75% and finish a test within 45 minutes, then you are ready to take your official test.

If you do not pass the practice tests satisfactorily and do not feel confident enough to sit your official test you should continue your study of the testable materials. If you do not have sufficient time left before your test to do more study, then you may be able to reschedule your test appointment. You can reschedule your test without charge up to seven days before the date. If you cancel your booking with less than seven days' notice, your booking fee will not be refunded.

3. Online tests

Once you've finished testing yourself using the questions in this book, you can go online and access further tests with our free subscription offer.

Visit **www.lifeintheuk.net/test** and register an account to redeem this offer.

WARNING: DO NOT MEMORISE QUESTIONS

The practice questions contained in this book are intended to help you assess your understanding of the study materials and check if you are ready to take the official test.

Do not prepare for the test by memorising the questions in this book.

All the questions are in the same format as the official test questions. But they are not identical to the questions in the official test. The Home Office regularly revises the wording of questions used in the Life in the UK Test.

It is very important that you fully read and understand the study materials before taking your test.

SEND US YOUR FEEDBACK

Our books have helped thousands of people pass the Life in the UK Test. So we're always delighted when we hear from our readers. You can send us your comments by visiting **www.lifeintheuk.net/feedback**

CHECKLIST

There are a lot of things that you need to remember to do for the Life in the UK Test. Avoid problems and get organised by completing this checklist.

☐ Test appointment booked

Book your test through the Life in the UK Test booking website **www.lituktestbooking.co.uk/lituk-web/** or by calling the Life in the UK Test Helpline on **0800 015 4245**.

Test Date   Time

Test Centre Address

Phone

☐ Finished reading study materials

☐ Completed all practice tests in this book

☐ Completed free online practice tests at **www.lifeintheuk.net**

☐ Checked latest tips and advice at **www.lifeintheuk.net**

☐ Checked your registered details exactly match your photo ID

☐ Checked your proof of address is valid and in date

☐ Confirmed test centre location and travel route

QUESTIONS TO EXPECT

All questions in the Life in the UK Test are multiple-choice. There are four different formats in which a question may be asked:

1. **Choose the one correct answer to the question from four options**

   ### *EXAMPLE*

   What important event in the development of women's rights happened in 1928?

   A Women were first given the right to vote

   B Women were given the right to vote at the same age as men

   C The first divorce laws were introduced

   D Women were allowed to keep their own earnings and property

2. **Choose two correct answers to the question from four options. You need BOTH parts to answer the question correctly**

   ### *EXAMPLE*

   Which TWO of the following are famous Paralympians?

   A Baroness Tanni Grey-Thompson

   B Dame Kelly Holmes

   C Jayne Torvill

   D Ellie Simmonds

3. **Decide whether a statement is true or false**

   ### *EXAMPLE*

   Is the statement below TRUE or FALSE?
   A newspaper's owner may try to influence government policy by running a campaign.

   A True

   B False

4. Choose the correct statement from two options

EXAMPLE

Which of these statements is correct?

 A Florence Nightingale is often regarded as the founder of modern nursing.

B Florence Nightingale pioneered the use of syringes in hospitals.

Working through the answers

When you start your test, make sure you read each question carefully. Make sure you understand it.

If you are confident that you know the correct answer, make your selection and move on to the next question.

It is vital that you select an answer for every question even if you are not confident that it is correct. There is a chance that even a guess will be correct! If you do this, make sure that you note the question number on your blank paper. It is possible that a question later in the test will help you to answer a question that you have found difficult.

Things to watch out for

Some questions may be worded so that an option may be a TRUE statement but not the CORRECT answer to the question being asked.

Be careful if questions and answers use words that are absolute. These words mean that the question or answer applies in all cases (e.g. *always*, *every*) or not at all (e.g. *never*).

EXAMPLE

Which of the following statements is correct?

 A There are a few members of Parliament who do not represent any of the main political parties.

B Members of Parliament always belong to a political party.

The second statement is absolute. There are no exceptions. This means the correct answer is A because, whether or not there are currently independent members of Parliament (MPs) in Parliament, there *can* be independent MPs in Parliament.

You also need to be careful of words that *moderate* a question or answer. When words such as *often, rarely, sometimes* and *usually* are used, this means that the question or answer is referring to something that is not always true.

EXAMPLE

Which of the following statements is correct?

A Magistrates usually don't get paid and do not need legal qualifications.

B Magistrates must be specially trained legal experts who have been solicitors for three years.

Whilst magistrates may be paid in some places, they usually work for free. Also, whilst they can have legal qualifications it is not compulsory. B is not correct in all cases, so the right answer is A.

Dates

You may get questions on dates. The study materials state you don't need to learn the dates of births and deaths, but you do have to know the dates of significant events.

EXAMPLE

When was the last successful invasion of England?

A 1066

B 1415

C 1642

D 1940

This question relates to the Norman invasion of 1066. You do need to know the dates of major events mentioned in the study materials.

EXAMPLE

Is the statement below TRUE or FALSE?
In the UK, people play practical jokes on each other on 1 April.

 A True

B False

You need to know which festivals and celebrations happen on which date. Questions may cover the patron saints of the UK, religious festivals and public holidays.

The study materials say that 'Questions are based on ALL parts of the handbook, but you will not need to remember dates of birth or death' (see *The values and principles of the UK*). You must understand, however, when key events happened, or when certain individuals lived. For example, you will not be asked a question such as 'What year was Isaac Newton born in?', though you could be asked 'Which scientist, born in 1643, discovered that white light is made up of the colours of the rainbow?'

Annual Events

The other exception with dates is annual events and festivals. Where something happens on the same date each year, such as Christmas or St George's Day, you must know the specific date. For moveable festivals such as Easter or Hannukah, you need to know in which months of the year they normally fall.

PRACTICE TEST 1

1   Which of the following statements is correct?

  A Many civilian volunteers helped the British Navy to rescue more than 300,000 men from the beaches around Dunkirk.

  B 300,000 men were rescued from the beaches around Dunkirk solely by British Navy ships.

2   Which king, who succeeded Henry VIII, died when he was 15 years old?

  A Edward VI

  B Charles I

  C Harold

  D Richard III

3   Is the statement below TRUE or FALSE?
Charles II marched into England with a Scottish army to reclaim his throne.

  A True

  B False

4   Which of the following statements is correct?

  A A bank holiday in the UK refers to banks being closed on that day.

  B A bank holiday in the UK happens each calendar month.

5   Which TWO of the following are famous British landmarks?

  A The London Eye

  B Mont Blanc

  C The Eden Project

  D The Smithsonian

6 **Which country of the UK is not represented on the Union Flag?**

- **A** Scotland
- **B** Wales
- **C** Northern Ireland
- **D** England

7 **Which of these people was a great British playwright?**

- **A** Sir Francis Drake
- **B** Geoffrey Chaucer
- **C** William Caxton
- **D** William Shakespeare

8 **Which of the following statements is correct?**

- **A** Refuges and shelters offer a safe place to stay for victims of domestic violence.
- **B** The Citizens Advice Bureau offers a safe place to stay for victims of domestic violence.

9 **When were the first professional football clubs formed?**

- **A** The Middle Ages
- **B** 17th Century
- **C** 19th Century
- **D** 20th Century

10 **Which of the following is a famous composer who wrote operas such as *Peter Grimes* and *Billy Budd*?**

- **A** Dame Zaha Hadid
- **B** Gustav Holst
- **C** Benjamin Britten
- **D** Henry Purcell

11 Which of the following statements is correct?

   A The UK was one of the founding members of the European Economic Community.

   B The UK only joined the European Economic Community in 1973.

12 Is the following statement TRUE or FALSE?
Volunteering and helping your community are important parts of being a good citizen.

   A True

   B False

13 How are local authorities funded?

   A By funding from central government only

   B By local taxes

   C By central government funding and by local taxes

   D Local authorities are unfunded

14 Is the statement below TRUE or FALSE?
Discrimination in the workplace is covered by criminal law.

   A True

   B False

15 Which of the following statements is correct?

   A Everyone pays National Insurance Contributions.

   B Most working people pay National Insurance Contributions.

16 Whom did William the Conqueror defeat at the Battle of Hastings in 1066?

   A King Cnut

   B Boudicca

   C Kenneth MacAlpin

   D King Harold

17 Which British novelist created the fictional detective Sherlock Holmes?

- **A** Sir Arthur Conan Doyle
- **B** Evelyn Waugh
- **C** Robert Louis Stevenson
- **D** Graham Greene

18 The judiciary is responsible for which TWO of the following?

- **A** Interpreting the law
- **B** Keeping order during political debates
- **C** Nominating peers
- **D** Making sure that trials are fair

19 Who chairs debates in the House of Commons?

- **A** The Leader of the Opposition
- **B** The Prime Minister
- **C** The Speaker
- **D** The Foreign Secretary

20 The first day of one notorious battle in 1916 resulted in 60,000 British casualties. What was this battle?

- **A** The Battle of the Somme
- **B** The Battle of the Bulge
- **C** The Battle of Agincourt
- **D** The Battle of the River Plate

21 **Which two of the following are British overseas territories?**

- **A** Jamaica
- **B** St Helena
- **C** Australia
- **D** The Falkland Islands

22 **Is the statement below TRUE or FALSE?**
Population growth in the UK has been faster in recent years, thanks in part to migration and longer life expectancy.

- **A** True
- **B** False

23 **How old do you have to be to buy alcohol in the UK?**

- **A** 16
- **B** 18
- **C** 20
- **D** 21

24 **Who is the patron saint of Scotland?**

- **A** St David
- **B** St George
- **C** St Patrick
- **D** St Andrew

ANSWERS: PRACTICE TEST 1

			Study material reference
1	A	Many civilian volunteers helped the British Navy to rescue more than 300,000 men from the beaches around Dunkirk.	p48–52
2	A	Edward VI	p22–4
3	A	True	p28–30
4	A	A bank holiday in the UK refers to banks being closed on that day.	p73
5	A	The London Eye	p95–103
	C	The Eden Project	
6	B	Wales	p40
7	D	William Shakespeare	p26
8	A	Refuges and shelters offer a safe place to stay for victims of domestic violence.	p136
9	C	19th Century	p76–7
10	C	Benjamin Britten	p79–81
11	B	The UK only joined the European Economic Community in 1973.	p124–5
12	A	True	p141
13	C	By central government funding and by local taxes	p115
14	B	False	p126–7
15	B	Most working people pay National Insurance Contributions.	p138–9
16	D	King Harold	p15–6
17	A	Sir Arthur Conan Doyle	p85–6
18	A	Interpreting the law	p129–30
	D	Making sure that trials are fair	
19	C	The Speaker	p111–2
20	A	The Battle of the Somme	p46–7
21	B	St Helena	p8
	D	The Falkland Islands	
22	A	True	p64–5
23	B	18	p126–7
24	D	St Andrew	p67–8

PRACTICE TEST 2

1   Which TWO of the following are British values based on?

   A Traditions

   B EU law

   C Party politics

   D History

2   MPs have a duty to serve and represent which of the following groups?

   A Their fellow MPs

   B Everyone in their constituency

   C Everyone in their constituency who voted for them

   D The House of Lords

3   Which of the following statements is correct?

   A Canals were built by the Victorians who wanted to take recreational boat trips.

   B During the Industrial Revolution, canals were built to link factories to cities and ports.

4   An attempt by which group to put James II's son on the throne instead of George I was quickly defeated?

   A French Huguenots

   B Scottish Jacobites

   C Irish Catholics

   D English Puritans

5   John Petts was a Welshman famous in which TWO of these areas of art?

  A Stained glass

  B Water colours

  C Engraving

  D Paintings of horses

6   Charles I was unwilling to reach an agreement with Parliament. Following his defeat in the Civil War, what happened to him?

  A He was exiled

  B He was executed

  C He was exonerated

  D He was excommunicated

7   Is the statement below TRUE or FALSE?
Following the Emancipation Act of 1833, the Royal Navy stopped slave ships from other countries and freed the slaves.

  A True

  B False

8   Is the statement below TRUE or FALSE?
In Ireland, during the 17th century, Protestant settlers took over land, known as 'plantations', from the Catholics.

  A True

  B False

9   Is the statement below TRUE or FALSE?
Some people rent land away from home called an allotment, where they can grow fruit and vegetables.

  A True

  B False

10 Which of the following statements is correct?

    A Most people live in towns and cities but much of Britain is still countryside.

    B Most people live in the countryside but much of Britain is covered by towns and cities.

11 During the reign of Henry VIII, which country of the union became formally united with England?

    A Ireland

    B Wales

    C Scotland

    D Northern Ireland

12 What sport is played in the UEFA Champions League?

    A Tennis

    B Rugby

    C Football

    D Cricket

13 Is the statement below TRUE or FALSE?
Norman French influenced the development of the English language as we know it today.

    A True

    B False

14 Which of the following statements is correct?

    A The attack on Normandy by Allied forces is often called D-Day.

    B D-Day was an Allied operation that attacked German forces in France by advancing through Spain.

15 **Which annual flower show in London exhibits garden designs from around the world?**

A South Bank

B Covent Garden

C Chelsea

D Kensington

16 **Where did the people of the Bronze Age bury their dead?**

A Wheelbarrows

B Round barrows

C Cathedrals

D Hill forts

17 **The right for every adult male and female to vote is usually known as what?**

A Universal balloting

B Universal democracy

C Universal voting rights

D Universal suffrage

18 **What event in 1851 took place at the Crystal Palace in Hyde Park and showed goods and exhibits from Britain and across the world?**

A The Great Exhibition

B The Great Show

C The Great Event

D The Great Occasion

19 **Sake Dean Mahomet opened which establishment in George Street, London in 1810?**

A Hindoostane Coffee House

B Pakistan Curry House

C Mahomet Coffee House

D Mahomet Shampoo Parlour

20 **Which of these is a Christmas tradition in the UK?**

A Eating chocolate eggs

B Having a barbecue

C Fireworks displays

D Decorating houses and trees

21 **Is the statement below TRUE or FALSE?**
Anne Boleyn was Henry VIII's fourth wife.

A True

B False

22 **Which of the following statements is correct?**

A Elizabeth I succeeded Bloody Mary to become Queen of England.

B Elizabeth I succeeded Henry VIII to become Queen of England.

23 **Who wrote musicals such as *Cats*, *The Phantom of the Opera* and *Evita*?**

A Sir Edward Elgar

B Gilbert and Sullivan

C Andrew Lloyd Webber

D Julian Lloyd Webber

24 **Is the statement below TRUE or FALSE?**
The MacDonald clan of Glencoe were massacred by William III.

A True

B False

ANSWERS: PRACTICE TEST 2

			Study material reference
1	A	Traditions	p2–3
	D	History	
2	B	Everyone in their constituency	p112
3	B	During the Industrial Revolution, canals were built to link factories to cities and ports.	p35–7
4	B	Scottish Jacobites	p34
5	A	Stained glass	p82–3
	C	Engraving	
6	B	He was executed	p28–30
7	A	True	p37–8
8	A	True	p27
9	A	True	p88–9
10	A	Most people live in towns and cities but much of Britain is still countryside.	p62–3
11	B	Wales	p22–4
12	C	Football	p76–7
13	A	True	p15–6
14	A	The attack on Normandy by Allied forces is often called D-Day.	p48–52
15	C	Chelsea	p84–5
16	B	Round barrows	p12–3
17	D	Universal suffrage	p43–4
18	A	The Great Exhibition	p41–2
19	A	Hindoostane Coffee House	p37
20	D	Decorating houses and trees	p69–70
21	B	False	p23
22	A	Elizabeth I succeeded Bloody Mary to become Queen of England.	p22–4
23	C	Andrew Lloyd Webber	p81–2
24	A	True	p31–2

PRACTICE TEST 3

1   Which of the following statements is correct?

A The Wimbledon Championships is an athletics tournament.

B The Wimbledon Championships is a tennis tournament.

2   The last successful foreign invasion of England was by which of the following?

A The Romans led by Julius Caesar

B The Romans led by Emperor Claudius

C The Vikings

D The Normans led by William

3   Is the statement below TRUE or FALSE?
Mary Peters was an author who was later made a Dame in recognition of her work promoting literacy.

A True

B False

4   Where does the UK Parliament sit?

A Westminster

B Downing Street

C Stormont

D Edinburgh Castle

5   Which of the following statements is correct?

A The 'Divine Right of Kings' meant English monarchs could only be chosen by the Pope.

B The 'Divine Right of Kings' meant English monarchs believed they were directly appointed by God to rule.

6   The repeal of the Corn Laws in 1846 was designed to do what?

- **A** Allow the import of cheap grain
- **B** Encourage British farmers to grow more grain
- **C** Increase the quality of bread
- **D** Introduce more efficient working practices on British farms

7   The Wars of the Roses were fought by the supporters of which TWO families in order to decide who should be king of England?

- **A** The House of Lancaster
- **B** The House of Windsor
- **C** The House of York
- **D** The House of Tudor

8   Which famous leader said the following:
'We shall fight on the beaches, we shall fight on the landing grounds, we shall fight in the fields and in the streets, we shall fight in the hills; we shall never surrender.'

- **A** Admiral Nelson
- **B** Winston Churchill
- **C** Clement Attlee
- **D** Oliver Cromwell

9   Which of the following statements is correct?

- **A** The police must always obey the law, unless Parliament grants an exemption.
- **B** The police must always obey the law.

10   Which of the following is an aim of the United Nations?

- **A** Protecting UK wildlife
- **B** Promoting international security
- **C** Teaching people English
- **D** Promoting free trade

11   How often is a General Election held?

    A   Every year

    B   At least every two years

    C   At least every four years

    D   At least every five years

12   Which of the following statements is correct?

    A   Oliver Cromwell became king of England after Parliament won the Civil War.

    B   After Parliament won the Civil War, England became a republic and Oliver Cromwell was named Lord Protector.

13   Which of the following statements is correct?

    A   The Black Death destroyed cereal crops, leading to a famine which killed many peasants.

    B   After the Black Death there were labour shortages and peasants began to demand higher wages.

14   What is the capital city of Northern Ireland?

    A   Belfast

    B   Dublin

    C   The Pale

    D   Edinburgh

15   What is New Year's Eve called in Scotland?

    A   Boxing Day

    B   Hogmanay

    C   Auld Lang Syne

    D   St Andrew's Day

16 Who or what were the 'clans'?

- **A** English lords
- **B** Welsh landowners
- **C** Prominent families in Scotland and Ireland
- **D** Prominent families in England and Wales

17 Who defeated James II at the Battle of the Boyne in 1690?

- **A** William III
- **B** William the Conqueror
- **C** Elizabeth I
- **D** Winston Churchill

18 What significant problem arose for Britain from trading and settlements overseas in the 19th century?

- **A** Conflict with other countries, particularly France
- **B** The Industrial Revolution made shipbuilding expensive
- **C** There was no plan or structure to the expansion
- **D** The Great Depression caused mass unemployment

19 Which British director made films including *The 39 Steps*?

- **A** Alfred Hitchcock
- **B** Charlie Chaplin
- **C** Ridley Scott
- **D** William Walton

20 Is the statement below TRUE or FALSE?
Members of the House of Lords are elected by a constituency.

   A True

   B False

21 Who wrote the novel *Lucky Jim*?

   A James Joyce

   B Sir Kingsley Amis

   C James Callaghan

   D Jimmy Tarbuck

22 Which of the following statements is correct?

   A The United Kingdom consists of England, Ireland, Scotland and Wales.

   B The United Kingdom consists of England, Scotland, Wales and Northern Ireland.

23 Which TWO of the following are core values of the Commonwealth?

   A The rule of law

   B Mutual dependency

   C Democracy

   D Discrimination against non-members

24 Which of the following is one of the Queen's important ceremonial roles?

   A To chair debates in Parliament

   B To write laws

   C To receive foreign ambassadors and high commissioners

   D To negotiate trade agreements with other countries

ANSWERS: PRACTICE TEST 3

			Study material reference
1	B	The Wimbledon Championships is a tennis tournament.	p78
2	D	The Normans led by William	p15–6
3	B	False	p57
4	A	Westminster	p8
5	B	The 'Divine Right of Kings' meant English monarchs believed they were directly appointed by God to rule.	p27–8
6	A	Allow the import of cheap grain	p41–2
7	A	The House of Lancaster	p21
	C	The House of York	
8	B	Winston Churchill	p50
9	B	The police must always obey the law.	p127–8
10	B	Promoting international security	p125
11	D	At least every five years	p112
12	B	After Parliament won the Civil War, England became a republic and Oliver Cromwell was named Lord Protector.	p28–30
13	B	After the Black Death there were labour shortages and peasants began to demand higher wages.	p17–8
14	A	Belfast	p62–3
15	B	Hogmanay	p72
16	C	Prominent families in Scotland and Ireland	p17–8
17	A	William III	p31–2
18	A	Conflict with other countries, particularly France	p35–7
19	A	Alfred Hitchcock	p90–1
20	B	False	p111
21	B	Sir Kingsley Amis	p86
22	B	The United Kingdom consists of England, Scotland, Wales and Northern Ireland.	p8
23	A	The rule of law	p123–4
	C	Democracy	
24	C	To receive foreign ambassadors and high commissioners	p107–9

PRACTICE TEST 4

1 Who introduced a system called feudalism to Britain?

- **A** Vikings
- **B** Jutes
- **C** Normans
- **D** Anglo-Saxons

2 Which of the following statements is correct?

- **A** A verdict of 'not proven' is possible in all UK courts.
- **B** A verdict of 'not proven' is only possible in Scottish courts.

3 Is the statement below TRUE or FALSE?
Jane Austen and Charles Dickens were both famous sculptors.

- **A** True
- **B** False

4 Which UNESCO World Heritage site includes the Roman forts of Housesteads and Vindolanda?

- **A** Snowdonia
- **B** The Trossachs National Park
- **C** Hadrian's Wall
- **D** The Giant's Causeway

5   Is the statement below TRUE or FALSE?
Adult citizens of all EU states may vote in General Elections.

   A True

   B False

6   After the Act of Union, Scotland was no longer an independent country. In which way was it still separate from the rest of Great Britain?

   A Hadrian's Wall stopped people travelling freely

   B It kept its own educational system

   C No one spoke English

   D It had its own monarch

7   Which of the following statements is correct?

   A A dog's owner is responsible for cleaning up after it in public places.

   B Local authorities employ people to clean up after dogs in public places.

8   Is the statement below TRUE or FALSE?
Richard Arkwright developed horse-driven spinning mills that used only one machine, increasing efficiency and production.

   A True

   B False

9   Which of these books did Graham Greene write?

   A *The Honorary Consul*

   B *George's Marvellous Medicine*

   C *Moby Dick*

   D *Brideshead Revisited*

10 Who were Elizabeth I's parents?

> **A** Henry VII and Elizabeth of York
>
> **B** Henry VIII and Catherine of Aragon
>
> **C** Henry VIII and Jane Seymour
>
> **D** Henry VIII and Anne Boleyn

11 In 1948 Aneurin (Nye) Bevan led the establishment of which of the following?

> **A** The Northern Ireland peace process
>
> **B** The Paralympics
>
> **C** The EEC
>
> **D** The National Health Service

12 What was the main source of employment in the UK before the Industrial Revolution?

> **A** Agriculture
>
> **B** The wool trade
>
> **C** Financial services
>
> **D** Canal building

13 Which of the following statements is correct?

> **A** The jet engine and radar were developed in Britain in the 1950s.
>
> **B** The jet engine and radar were developed in Britain in the 1930s.

14 Is the statement below TRUE or FALSE?
By around AD 600, Anglo-Saxon kingdoms were established in Britain.

> **A** True
>
> **B** False

15 In 1649, England was declared a republic. What was it called?

- **A** The Commonwealth
- **B** The People's Republic
- **C** Cromwell's Republic
- **D** Great Britain

16 Which TWO of the following were members of the Royal Society?

- **A** John Middleton
- **B** Samuel Pepys
- **C** Sir Edmond Halley
- **D** Sir Isaac Newton

17 Is the statement below TRUE or FALSE?
It is acceptable in the UK to discriminate against people because of their sexual orientation.

- **A** True
- **B** False

18 Queen Elizabeth II is the head of state for which TWO of the following?

- **A** The United Kingdom
- **B** The European Union
- **C** NATO
- **D** Many Commonwealth countries

19 Who was the first Prime Minister?

- **A** William Wilberforce
- **B** Sir Robert Walpole
- **C** Benjamin Disraeli
- **D** William Gladstone

20 **A snack made from flour, dried fruits and spices, and served either hot or cold is which of the following?**

A A Scottish bun

B An English muffin

C An Irish pie

D A Welsh cake

21 **What is the name of the famous horse-race held near Liverpool?**

A Grand Chase

B Grand Derby

C Steeplechase

D Grand National

22 **NATO is a group of North American and European countries which have agreed to do which TWO of the following?**

A Promote peace between member countries

B Promote traditional culture

C To protect each other when under attack

D To allow the free movement of people across borders

23 **Is the statement below TRUE or FALSE?**
Commercial expansion and prosperity in the 18th century were sustained in part by the booming slave trade.

A True

B False

24 **Is the statement below TRUE or FALSE?**
You have to be 16 or over to buy alcohol in a pub or nightclub.

A True

B False

ANSWERS: PRACTICE TEST 4

			Study material reference
1	C	Normans	p17–8
2	B	A verdict of 'not proven' is only possible in Scottish courts.	p130–3
3	B	False	p86
4	C	Hadrian's Wall	p13
5	B	False	p120
6	B	It kept its own educational system	p34
7	A	A dog's owner is responsible for cleaning up after it in public places.	p94
8	A	True	p35–7
9	A	*The Honorary Consul*	p85–6
10	D	Henry VIII and Anne Boleyn	p22–4
11	D	The National Health Service	p52–4
12	A	Agriculture	p35–7
13	B	The jet engine and radar were developed in Britain in the 1930s.	p56–7
14	A	True	p13–5
15	A	The Commonwealth	p28–30
16	C	Sir Edmond Halley	p30–1
	D	Sir Isaac Newton	
17	B	False	p136
18	A	The United Kingdom	p107–9
	D	Many Commonwealth countries	
19	B	Sir Robert Walpole	p34
20	D	A Welsh cake	p89–90
21	D	Grand National	p77
22	A	Promote peace between member countries	p125
	C	To protect each other when under attack	
23	A	True	p37–8
24	B	False	p93

PRACTICE TEST 5

1   Is the statement below TRUE or FALSE?
*The police do not need to protect and help
people who are not UK citizens.*

    A True

    B False

2   Is the statement below TRUE or FALSE?
The Channel Islands and the Isle of Man are part of the UK.

    A True

    B False

3   Is the statement below TRUE or FALSE?
*The Puritans agreed with the religious reforms of the
Church of England introduced by Charles I.*

    A True

    B False

**4   Which of Henry VIII's wives was executed after being accused
of taking lovers?**

    A Jane Seymour

    B Mary Stuart

    C Elizabeth of York

    D Catherine Howard

5   How old must you be to stand for election as an MP?

    A 16

    B 18

    C 21

    D There is no minimum age limit

6 Sir Anthony Van Dyck was famous as which of the following?

A Actor

B Painter

C Sculptor

D Composer

7 Which of the following takes place on 14 February every year?

A St Christopher's Day

B St George's Day

C Valentine's Day

D All Saints Day

8 Which of the following statements is correct?

A Chequers is the Prime Minister's country house.

B Chequers is the Prime Minister's house in London.

9 Where did Florence Nightingale establish the Nightingale School for Nurses in 1860?

A St Thomas' Hospital, London

B Addenbrooke's Hospital, Cambridge

C St James's University Hospital, Leeds

D Prince Philip Hospital, Llanelli

10 Is the statement below TRUE or FALSE?
The Highland Clearances occurred in Wales.

A True

B False

11 **Ian McEwan, Hilary Mantel and Julian Barnes have all won which literary prize?**

- **A** The Turner Prize
- **B** The Man Booker Prize
- **C** The Nobel Prize in Literature
- **D** The Mercury Prize

12 **For much of the Stone Age, Britain was connected to the continent by what?**

- **A** A bridge
- **B** A land bridge
- **C** A glacier
- **D** A tunnel

13 **Which of the following statements is correct?**

- **A** Pantomimes are usually based on fairy stories.
- **B** Pantomimes are usually based on famous events from history.

14 **Which of the following statements is correct?**

- **A** Elizabeth I established a balance between Catholics and Protestants by not persecuting either group.
- **B** Elizabeth I reduced the powers of the House of Commons.

15 **The National Assembly makes laws for Wales in which of the following areas?**

- **A** Defence
- **B** Foreign policy
- **C** Immigration
- **D** Health and social services

16 **Is the statement below TRUE or FALSE?**
After the Second World War, the British government encouraged workers from Ireland and other parts of Europe to come to the UK and help to rebuild Britain.

A True

B False

---

17 **Is the statement below TRUE or FALSE?**
In the Middle Ages, England's system of 'common law' was established by referring to previous decisions and tradition.

A True

B False

---

18 **Who became Prime Minister in May 2010?**

A David Cameron

B Nick Clegg

C Ed Miliband

D Nigel Farage

---

19 **Which Hindu and Sikh festival is normally celebrated in October or November every year?**

A Diwali

B Vaisakhi

C Eid ul Adha

D Hannukah

---

20 **Is the statement below TRUE or FALSE?**
The small claims procedure is an informal way for people to settle minor disputes.

A True

B False

21 What event is commemorated on 5 November every year?

- **A** England's World Cup victory of 1966
- **B** The end of the First World War
- **C** A plot to blow up the Houses of Parliament
- **D** The Queen's birthday

22 What is Ridley Scott famous for?

- **A** Directing films
- **B** Theatre production
- **C** Conducting orchestras
- **D** Singing as an operatic tenor

23 Is the statement below TRUE or FALSE?
The UK is a parliamentary democracy.

- **A** True
- **B** False

24 Which of the following statements is correct?

- **A** Murder, assault and theft are crimes.
- **B** Murder, assault and theft are examples of civil disputes.

ANSWERS: PRACTICE TEST 5

			Study material reference
1	B	False	p127–8
2	B	False	p8
3	B	False	p28
4	D	Catherine Howard	p23
5	B	18	p114
6	B	Painter	p82–3
7	C	Valentine's Day	p72–3
8	A	Chequers is the Prime Minister's country house.	p113
9	A	St Thomas' Hospital, London	p43
10	B	False	p34–5
11	B	The Man Booker Prize	p85–6
12	B	A land bridge	p12–3
13	A	Pantomimes are usually based on fairy stories.	p81–2
14	A	Elizabeth I established a balance between Catholics and Protestants by not persecuting either group.	p24–5
15	D	Health and social services	p115–9
16	A	True	p54
17	A	True	p18–9
18	A	David Cameron	p60
19	A	Diwali	p70–1
20	A	True	p133–4
21	C	A plot to blow up the Houses of Parliament	p72–3
22	A	Directing films	p90–1
23	A	True	p110
24	A	Murder, assault and theft are crimes.	p126–7

PRACTICE TEST 6

1 **Which period of British history saw the emergence of a national culture and identity?**

- **A** The Bronze Age
- **B** The Middle Ages
- **C** The Victorian period
- **D** The Tudor period

2 **What is the capital city of the UK?**

- **A** Birmingham
- **B** Liverpool
- **C** London
- **D** Sheffield

3 **Is the statement below TRUE or FALSE?**
Sir Steve Redgrave was the first man in the world to run a mile in under four minutes.

- **A** True
- **B** False

4 **Is the statement below TRUE or FALSE?**
Between 1853 and 1913 very few British citizens left the UK to settle overseas.

- **A** True
- **B** False

5 **Is the statement below TRUE or FALSE?**
Shakespeare wrote the line 'The darling buds of May'.

- **A** True
- **B** False

6 **Is the statement below TRUE or FALSE?**
Sir Ian Botham captained the England rugby team.

A True

B False

7 **Where did the Boer War take place?**

A South Africa

B France

C England

D Turkey

8 **Richard Arkwright is remembered for developing which of the following?**

A Radar systems

B Efficient and profitable factories

C Universal suffrage

D The World Wide Web

9 **Henry VIII took which title in relation to Ireland?**

A Head

B King

C Lieutenant

D Commander

10 **Which of the following statements is correct?**

A During the 16th century the Scottish Parliament welcomed the authority of the Pope.

B During the 16th century the Scottish Parliament abolished the authority of the Pope.

11 Which of the following statements is correct?

   A A Magistrates' Court deals with only the most serious criminal cases.

   B A Magistrates' Court deals with minor criminal offences.

12 Which of the following is an important festival for Muslims in the UK?

   A Hannukah

   B Vaisakhi

   C Eid al-Fitr

   D Hogmanay

13 The National Eisteddfod is a major cultural festival which takes place in which country?

   A England

   B Scotland

   C Wales

   D Northern Ireland

14 Is the statement below TRUE or FALSE?
The threat of Viking attack caused the peoples in the north to unite, and begin to use the term Scotland to describe that country.

   A True

   B False

15 What are the BAFTAs the British equivalent of?

   A The Victoria Cross

   B The Man Booker Prize

   C The Laurence Olivier Awards

   D The Oscars

16 Which famous British novelist wrote *Brighton Rock*?

- **A** Kingsley Amis
- **B** Graham Greene
- **C** Evelyn Waugh
- **D** Arthur Conan Doyle

17 Who is the ceremonial head of the Commonwealth?

- **A** The Prime Minister
- **B** The President of the USA
- **C** The Queen
- **D** The Prince of Wales

18 The French Wars ended in 1815 when Napoleon was defeated by the Duke of Wellington at which battle?

- **A** Battle of Waterloo
- **B** Battle of Trafalgar
- **C** Battle of Ostend
- **D** Battle of Naseby

19 Which Anglo-Saxon poem tells of its hero's battles against monsters?

- **A** *Beowulf*
- **B** *The Fight at Finnsburh*
- **C** *Waldere*
- **D** *Deor*

20 Which of the following statements is correct?

- **A** The UK experienced high levels of employment during the Great Depression of the 1930s.
- **B** During the Great Depression of the 1930s parts of the UK experienced mass unemployment.

21 **To apply to become a permanent resident or citizen of the UK, you will need to be able to do which TWO of the following?**

  A Speak and read English

  B Speak Welsh

  C Have a good understanding of life in the UK

  D Speak more than one language

22 **Which of the following is a famous British film?**

  A *Passport to Paddington*

  B *Passport to Portsmouth*

  C *Passport to Panama*

  D *Passport to Pimlico*

23 **In a Crown Court, who decides what the penalty will be, in the case of a 'guilty' verdict?**

  A A solicitor

  B The judge

  C The jury

  D A police officer

24 **Every MP represents which of the following?**

  A A constituency

  B A county

  C A city

  D Just the people who voted for them

ANSWERS: PRACTICE TEST 6

			Study material reference
1	B	The Middle Ages	p19–21
2	C	London	p62–3
3	B	False	p74–5
4	B	False	p41
5	A	True	p26
6	B	False	p74–5
7	A	South Africa	p45
8	B	Efficient and profitable factories	p36
9	B	King	p27
10	B	During the 16th century the Scottish Parliament abolished the authority of the Pope.	p25
11	B	A Magistrates' Court deals with minor criminal offences.	p130–3
12	C	Eid al-Fitr	p70–1
13	C	Wales	p79–81
14	A	True	p15
15	D	The Oscars	p90–1
16	B	Graham Greene	p86
17	C	The Queen	p123–4
18	A	Battle of Waterloo	p38–9
19	A	*Beowulf*	p86–8
20	B	During the Great Depression of the 1930s parts of the UK experienced mass unemployment.	p48
21	A	Speak and read English	p3–4
	C	Have a good understanding of life in the UK	
22	D	*Passport to Pimlico*	p90–1
23	B	The judge	p130–3
24	A	A constituency	p110

PRACTICE TEST 7

1   **Who were the Huguenots, who came to the UK in the
18th century to escape religious persecution?**

   A   Roman Catholics

   B   French Catholics

   C   Dutch Protestants

   D   French Protestants

2   **Which of the following statements is correct?**

   A   Employment opportunities for women are much
greater now than they were in the past.

   B   Men now work in less varied jobs than they did in the past.

3   **Who wrote the poem *The Tyger*?**

   A   William Wordsworth

   B   William Blake

   C   William Shakespeare

   D   William Wallace

4   **Which of the following statements is correct?**

   A   Robert Burns was a poet who wrote only in Scots language.

   B   Robert Burns is a poet who wrote in Scots, English and a
combination of both.

5   **Is the statement below TRUE or FALSE?**
*The Prime Minister has had the power to
nominate life peers since 1958.*

   A   True

   B   False

6 Which of the following statements is correct?

A All the national saints' days are celebrated but only in Scotland and Northern Ireland are they official holidays.

B All the national saints' days are celebrated but only in England and Wales are they official holidays.

7 Which organisation did the UK vote to leave in a referendum on 23 June 2016?

A United Nations

B Commonwealth

C European Union

D NATO

8 Which of the following will help you get along with your neighbours?

A Only putting rubbish and recycling out on collection days

B Having an untidy garden

C Making lots of noise, especially late at night

D Only introducing yourself to them after a year

9 Is the statement below TRUE or FALSE?
Cricket is the UK's most popular sport.

A True

B False

10 In which modern-day country was the composer George Frederick Handel born?

A England

B America

C Russia

D Germany

11 **The mass production of steel during the Industrial Revolution led to the development of which TWO industries?**

- **A** Railways
- **B** Shipbuilding
- **C** House-building
- **D** Agriculture

12 **Is the statement below TRUE or FALSE?**
There has been a Welsh Assembly and a Scottish Parliament since 1999.

- **A** True
- **B** False

13 **Is the statement below TRUE or FALSE?**
France was the first country to industrialise on a large scale.

- **A** True
- **B** False

14 **How often is Prime Minister's Questions held?**

- **A** Every day
- **B** Every day whilst Parliament is in session
- **C** Every week
- **D** Every week whilst Parliament is in session

15 **Which of the following statements is correct?**

- **A** People in the UK are living longer than ever before.
- **B** The average lifespan for UK residents is steadily decreasing.

16 Is the statement below TRUE or FALSE?
Thanks to its position as the world's leading industrial nation during the 1800s, Britain was responsible for producing half of the world's coal, iron and cotton cloth.

- **A** True
- **B** False

17 The Royal Society was formed to promote what?

- **A** Astrology
- **B** Natural knowledge
- **C** Art
- **D** Music

18 What is Charles Dickens famous for?

- **A** Film directing
- **B** Designing furniture
- **C** Writing novels
- **D** Painting

19 Which TWO events happened to the church in England following the restoration of Charles II?

- **A** The Church of England was restored as the official church
- **B** The Puritans and Roman Catholics were kept out of power
- **C** The Puritans grew in strength and number
- **D** The Church of England was suppressed

20 What is it traditional to do on 1 April in the UK?

- **A** Play musical instruments in the street
- **B** Play jokes on each other
- **C** Hunt for eggs
- **D** Make pancakes

21 **Is the statement below TRUE or FALSE?**
You must always tell a canvasser how you intend to vote.

   A True

   B False

22 **Which of the following statements is correct?**

   A Margaret Thatcher was the UK's first female Prime Minister.

   B Margaret Thatcher was the UK's second female Prime Minister.

23 **Which of the following statements is correct?**

   A Thomas Chippendale was an 18th century designer of furniture.

   B Sir Terence Conran was a 18th century designer of furniture.

24 **Is the statement below TRUE or FALSE?**
*The Bill of Rights confirmed the rights of Parliament
and the limits of the king's power.*

   A True

   B False

ANSWERS: PRACTICE TEST 7

			Study material reference
1	D	French Protestants	p34
2	A	Employment opportunities for women are much greater now than they were in the past.	p65–6
3	B	William Blake	p86–8
4	B	Robert Burns is a poet who wrote in Scots, English and a combination of both.	p35
5	A	True	p111
6	A	All the national saints' days are celebrated but only in Scotland and Northern Ireland are they official holidays.	p67–8
7	C	European Union	p124–5
8	A	Only putting rubbish and recycling out on collection days	p141
9	B	False	p76–7
10	D	Germany	p79–81
11	A	Railways	p35–7
	B	Shipbuilding	
12	A	True	p115–9
13	B	False	p35–7
14	D	Every week whilst Parliament is in session	p114
15	A	People in the UK are living longer than ever before.	p65
16	A	True	p41–2
17	B	Natural knowledge	p30–1
18	C	Writing novels	p85–6
19	A	The Church of England was restored as the official church	p30–1
	B	The Puritans and Roman Catholics were kept out of power	
20	B	Play jokes on each other	p72–3
21	B	False	p143
22	A	Margaret Thatcher was the UK's first female Prime Minister.	p58–9
23	A	Thomas Chippendale was an 18th century designer of furniture.	p85
24	A	True	p33

PRACTICE TEST 8

1   **The Chancellor of the Exchequer is responsible for which area of government policy?**

   A Health

   B The economy

   C Defence

   D Immigration

2   **The Scottish Parliament can make laws in which of the following areas?**

   A Health

   B All taxes

   C Social security

   D Immigration

3   **Which international organisation, of which the UK is a member, was set up to promote international peace and security?**

   A FIFA

   B World Health Organisation

   C The United Nations

   D The Eisteddfod

4   **The Industrial Revolution saw the rapid growth of which of the following in the 18th and 19th centuries?**

   A Agriculture

   B Democracy

   C Population

   D Industry

5 **Which king famously hid in an oak tree after escaping from the Battle of Worcester?**

⬭ **A** Edward I

⬭ **B** Charles II

⬭ **C** John

⬭ **D** George II

6 **Which TWO of the following are famous British sportsmen or women?**

⬭ **A** Baroness Tanni-Grey Thompson

⬭ **B** Mary Quant

⬭ **C** David Weir

⬭ **D** William Beveridge

7 **Which statement describes 'party politics' during the reign of William and Mary?**

⬭ **A** There were two main groups, the Liberals and the Conservatives.

⬭ **B** There were two main groups, the Tories and the Whigs.

8 **Which of the following is the job of the police?**

⬭ **A** To prosecute someone for being in debt

⬭ **B** To evict noisy tenants

⬭ **C** Representing clients in court

⬭ **D** To protect life and property

9 **Is the statement below TRUE or FALSE?**
All Acts of Parliament are made in the name of the Prime Minister.

⬭ **A** True

⬭ **B** False

10 Why was Parliament still some way from being a modern democracy after the Glorious Revolution?

    A Only bishops were able to vote

    B Only men who owned property of a certain value could vote

    C Only women were allowed to vote

    D Parliament took control of who could be monarch

11 What currency is used in the UK?

    A Euro

    B Dollar

    C Pound sterling

    D Ruble

12 Which of the following said *'I have nothing to offer but blood, toil, tears and sweat'*?

    A Charles II

    B Margaret Thatcher

    C Robert Browning

    D Winston Churchill

13 Which TWO of the following are freedoms citizens and permanent residents of the UK should respect?

    A Freedom of speech

    B Half-day off work on Friday

    C Freedom from unfair discrimination

    D Free heating during winter

14 In which city is the Scottish Parliament based?

    A Sheffield

    B Edinburgh

    C Glasgow

    D Cardiff

15 **Which Scottish poet wrote *The Bruce* about the Battle of Bannockburn?**

- **A** Robert Burns
- **B** John Barbour
- **C** Geoffrey Chaucer
- **D** John Milton

16 **Which of the following statements is correct?**

- **A** During Queen Victoria's reign the middle classes became increasingly significant.
- **B** During Queen Victoria's reign the size and influence of the British middle class shrank.

17 **Which Nobel Prize winning author of *The Jungle Book* lived in India and the USA, as well as the UK?**

- **A** JG Ballard
- **B** Jane Austen
- **C** Evelyn Waugh
- **D** Rudyard Kipling

18 **The Six Nations Championship is associated with which sport?**

- **A** Football
- **B** Cricket
- **C** Tennis
- **D** Rugby Union

19 **Who wrote the poem *She Walks in Beauty*?**

- **A** Sir John Betjeman
- **B** Sir Walter de la Mare
- **C** Elizabeth Browning
- **D** Lord Byron

20 Is the statement below TRUE or FALSE?
    The Education Act of 1944 is often called The Butler Act and introduced free secondary education in England and Wales.

    A True

    B False

21 Is the statement below TRUE or FALSE?
    The UK government has never used its power to suspend a devolved assembly.

    A True

    B False

22 Which of these films was directed by David Lean?

    A *Women in Love*

    B *Four Weddings and a Funeral*

    C *The Killing Fields*

    D *Brief Encounter*

23 What is the common name for the Yeoman Warders at the Tower of London?

    A Pikestaff

    B Queen's Men

    C Crown Guards

    D Beefeaters

24 Is the statement below TRUE or FALSE?
    In England, a mayor is always elected.

    A True

    B False

ANSWERS: PRACTICE TEST 8

			Study material reference
1	B	The economy	p113–4
2	A	Health	p115–9
3	C	The United Nations	p125
4	D	Industry	p35–7
5	B	Charles II	p28–30
6	A	Baroness Tanni-Grey Thompson	p74–5
	C	David Weir	
7	B	There were two main groups, the Tories and the Whigs.	p33
8	D	To protect life and property	p127–8
9	B	False	p107–9
10	B	Only men who owned property of a certain value could vote	p33
11	C	Pound sterling	p64
12	D	Winston Churchill	p50
13	A	Freedom of speech	p2–3
	C	Freedom from unfair discrimination	
14	B	Edinburgh	p115–9
15	B	John Barbour	p19–21
16	A	During Queen Victoria's reign the middle classes became increasingly significant.	p41
17	D	Rudyard Kipling	p45
18	D	Rugby Union	p77
19	D	Lord Byron	p86–8
20	A	True	p52–4
21	B	False	p115–9
22	D	*Brief Encounter*	p90–1
23	D	Beefeaters	p95–103
24	B	False	p115

PRACTICE TEST 9

1   Which of the following is a famous British television series?

   A *Touching the Void*

   B *Lord of the Rings*

   C *In Which We Serve*

   D *Monty Python's Flying Circus*

2   What was inscribed on some Iron Age coins?

   A Dates

   B Values

   C Names of Iron Age kings

   D Names of Iron Age settlements

3   During the 16th century which TWO factors predominantly led to a bloody rebellion by the Irish chieftains?

   A Extreme poverty and famine

   B The imposition of English laws on land inheritance

   C High taxes on landowners

   D The imposition of Protestantism

4   Which of the following statements is correct?

   A Visitors are not allowed in the Senedd.

   B The Senedd is an open building and visitors may book tours.

5   Which of the following statements is correct?

   A Every person in the UK requires a television licence.

   B Every household in the UK which has a television or device which receives television programmes must have a television licence.

6 **Which TWO of these countries did poet and author Rudyard Kipling spend time living in?**

A India

B Japan

C Fiji

D USA

7 **Is the statement below TRUE or FALSE?**
The Canterbury Tales *was one of the first books to be printed by William Caxton.*

A True

B False

8 **Acts of Parliament in 1870 and 1882 awarded which right to women?**

A The right to join the armed forces

B The right to work

C The right to attend university

D The right to keep their own earnings and property after marriage

9 **During the early 1970s, Britain admitted 28,000 people of Indian origin who had been forced to leave where?**

A The West Indies

B South Africa

C China

D Uganda

10 **To go into a betting shop or casino, you have to be what age?**

A 15

B 16

C 17

D 18

11 Which of these is a Gilbert and Sullivan comic opera?

- **A** *Evita*
- **B** *Jesus Christ Superstar*
- **C** *The Mikado*
- **D** *Cats*

12 Which battle does the Bayeux Tapestry commemorate?

- **A** Battle of Hastings
- **B** Battle of Bosworth Field
- **C** Battle of Bannockburn
- **D** Battle of Bayeux

13 Which of the following is covered by criminal law?

- **A** Drunk and disorderly behaviour
- **B** Disputes with your landlord
- **C** Employment issues such as unfair dismissal
- **D** Debt

14 Which of the following statements is correct?

- **A** In 1640, Puritan MPs didn't agree with Charles I's policies and refused to give him money.
- **B** Charles I was a famous Puritan, who advocated strict and simple religious doctrine and worship.

15 What happens at a polling station or polling place?

- **A** The census is collected
- **B** People vote in elections
- **C** Taxes are collected
- **D** People take their driving test

16 Which of the following statements is correct?

- **A** Big Ben refers to the great bell of the clock at the Houses of Parliament.
- **B** Big Ben is a novel written by Sir Kingsley Amis.

17 Around which structure in London is the Remembrance Day service usually held?

- **A** The statue of Eros in Piccadilly Circus
- **B** Nelson's Column in Trafalgar Square
- **C** The London Eye
- **D** The Cenotaph in Whitehall

18 Which of the following statements is correct?

- **A** Dogs in public places must wear a muzzle.
- **B** Dogs in public places must wear a collar showing the owner's name and address.
- **C** Cats in public places must wear a collar.
- **D** All dog owners must have a licence to keep their pets.

19 Which one of the following is one of the purposes of the National Citizen Service programme?

- **A** To support the police
- **B** To train young people for the army
- **C** To help secure Britain's borders
- **D** To give young people a chance to enjoy outdoor activities

20 Which king annexed Wales to the Crown of England with the Statute of Rhuddlan?

- **A** Charles I
- **B** Harold
- **C** Henry VIII
- **D** Edward I

21 Which of the following statements is correct?

   A Colonists in North America were well educated and interested in ideas of liberty.

   B Colonists in North America were poorly educated and uninterested in politics.

22 Which famous monarch spent much of her childhood in France and was at the centre of a power struggle on her return?

   A Mary, Queen of Scots

   B Elizabeth I

   C George I

   D George II

23 The UK has what kind of monarchy?

   A Democratic

   B Constitutional

   C Provisional

   D Absolute

24 Is the statement below TRUE or FALSE?
The candidate who wins the most votes in a constituency is elected as an MP.

   A True

   B False

ANSWERS: PRACTICE TEST 9

			Study material reference
1	D	*Monty Python's Flying Circus*	p91–2
2	C	Names of Iron Age kings	p12–3
3	B	The imposition of English laws on land inheritance	p22–4
	D	The imposition of Protestantism	
4	B	The Senedd is an open building and visitors may book tours.	p122–3
5	B	Every household in the UK which has a television or device which receives television programmes must have a television licence.	p92–3
6	A	India	p45
	D	USA	
7	A	True	p19–21
8	D	The right to keep their own earnings and property after marriage	p43–4
9	D	Uganda	p55
10	D	18	p93–4
11	C	*The Mikado*	p81–2
12	A	Battle of Hastings	p15–6
13	A	Drunk and disorderly behaviour	p126–7
14	A	In 1640, Puritan MPs didn't agree with Charles I's policies and refused to give him money.	p28
15	B	People vote in elections	p121
16	A	Big Ben refers to the great bell of the clock at the Houses of Parliament.	p95–103
17	D	The Cenotaph in Whitehall	p72–3
18	B	Dogs in public places must wear a collar showing the owner's name and address.	p94
19	D	To give young people a chance to enjoy outdoor activities	p144–6
20	D	Edward I	p17
21	A	Colonists in North America were well educated and interested in ideas of liberty.	p38
22	A	Mary, Queen of Scots	p25
23	B	Constitutional	p107–9
24	A	True	p112

PRACTICE TEST 10

1   The first farmers probably came to Britain from where?

   A Norway

   B South-east Europe

   C North America

   D North-west Europe

2   Which of the following statements is correct?

   A The UK has only hosted the Olympic games once, in 2012.

   B The UK hosted the Olympic Games in 1908, 1948 and 2012.

3   Is the statement below TRUE or FALSE?
   The High Court and the Court of Session hear the most serious civil cases.

   A True

   B False

4   Is the statement below TRUE or FALSE?
   A jump jet capable of taking off and landing vertically was developed in the UK, and was called the Falcon.

   A True

   B False

5   What is a Yorkshire pudding?

   A A caramel-flavoured dessert

   B Meat and potato in a pastry

   C Batter cooked in the oven

   D Apple and pears with custard

6 **Scotland changed in which TWO ways after the Battle of Culloden?**

    A Chieftains became landlords if they had the favour of the English king

    B Chieftains took control of the land away from the English king

    C Clansmen became tenants who had to pay for the land they used

    D The clans were entirely destroyed

7 **Is the statement below TRUE or FALSE?**
The Domesday Book no longer exists. It was destroyed at the end of the Norman Conquest.

    A True

    B False

8 **Which evangelical Christian and member of Parliament helped to change the laws on slavery?**

    A William Pitt

    B William Walpole

    C William Wallace

    D William Wilberforce

9 **Which of the following is a famous London building built in the 19th-century 'gothic' style?**

    A Westminster Cathedral

    B St Pancras Station

    C St James's Palace

    D St Paul's Cathedral

10 **Is the statement below TRUE or FALSE?**
At the beginning of the Middle Ages, England ruled Ireland.

    A True

    B False

11 **Which of the following statements is correct?**

A The cabinet's decisions often have to be debated or approved by Parliament.

B The cabinet's decisions must always be debated or approved by Parliament.

12 **Who became queen after the death of Edward VI?**

A Mary

B Victoria

C Elizabeth II

D Anne

13 **Which of the following statements is correct?**

A The Romans built roads, public buildings and created a structure of law.

B The Romans unified the whole of the British Isles.

14 **What do you accept and agree to respect when you become a permanent resident of the UK?**

A Catholic beliefs and values

B The right to be tried for crimes in your country of origin

C Traditions of the UK

D Protestant beliefs and values

15 **Is the statement below TRUE or FALSE?**
The Home Office selects who becomes a Police and Crime Commissioner (PCC).

A True

B False

16 How can you place your name on the electoral register?

  A By contacting your MP

  B By contacting your local electoral registration office

  C By contacting your MEP

  D By contacting your library

17 Is the following statement TRUE or FALSE?
Queen Victoria's reign ended in 1952, and
she was succeeded by Elizabeth II.

  A True

  B False

18 The Archbishop of Canterbury can most
accurately be described as what?

  A The spiritual leader of the Church of England

  B The political leader of the Church of England

  C The administrative leader of the Church of England

  D The financial leader of the Church of England

19 Is the statement below TRUE or FALSE?
The Welsh Assembly has limited power to make laws,
but considerable control over public services.

  A True

  B False

20 Which of the following statements is correct?

  A The House of Commons may overrule the House of Lords.

  B The House of Commons may never overrule the House of Lords.

21 What were *The Canterbury Tales*?

A A book of Christian doctrine

B A series of poems

C A Royal Charter

D A story about Canterbury Cathedral

22 Which of the following statements is correct?

A The UK's constitution is unwritten.

B The UK's constitution was originally a single document, now on display in the British Library.

23 Which TWO of the following have the right to vote to elect members of Parliament?

A Adults who have been granted an indefinite right to remain in the UK

B Adults who were born British citizens

C Adults who have been given a visa to study in the UK

D Adults who are naturalised citizens of the UK

24 Which of the following provide legal advice, normally for a fee?

A Judges

B Magistrates

C Solicitors

D The police

ANSWERS: PRACTICE TEST 10

			Study material reference
1	B	South-east Europe	p12–3
2	B	The UK hosted the Olympic Games in 1908, 1948 and 2012.	p74–5
3	A	True	p133–4
4	B	False	p56–7
5	C	Batter cooked in the oven	p90
6	A	Chieftains became landlords if they had the favour of the English king	p34–5
	C	Clansmen became tenants who had to pay for the land they used	
7	B	False	p15–6
8	D	William Wilberforce	p37–8
9	B	St Pancras Station	p84–5
10	B	False	p17
11	A	The cabinet's decisions often have to be debated or approved by Parliament.	p113–4
12	A	Mary	p22–4
13	A	The Romans built roads, public buildings and created a structure of law.	p13
14	C	Traditions of the UK	p2–3
15	B	False	p127–8
16	B	By contacting your local electoral registration office	p120–1
17	B	False	p41
18	A	The spiritual leader of the Church of England	p67
19	A	True	p59
20	A	The House of Commons may overrule the House of Lords.	p111
21	B	A series of poems	p19–21
22	A	The UK's constitution is unwritten.	p107
23	B	Adults who were born British citizens	p120
	D	Adults who are naturalised citizens of the UK	
24	C	Solicitors	p134–5

PRACTICE TEST 11

1 **Where would the Children's Hearings System deal with cases of children or young people accused of an offence?**

- **A** Northern Ireland
- **B** Wales
- **C** England
- **D** Scotland

2 **Areas of protected countryside that everyone can visit and where people live, work and look after the landscape are called which of the following?**

- **A** Greenfield sites
- **B** Country estates
- **C** National parks
- **D** Moorland

3 **Is the statement below TRUE or FALSE?**
In 55 BC, Julius Caesar led a Roman invasion of Britain.

- **A** True
- **B** False

4 **What was the Spanish Armada?**

- **A** A fleet of Spanish ships
- **B** A Spanish princess
- **C** A treaty with Spain
- **D** The Spanish Army

5 **Is the statement below TRUE or FALSE?**
Dame Judi Dench, Colin Firth and Sir Anthony
Hopkins are all actors who have won Oscars.

A True

B False

6 **The first people lived in Britain during which period?**

A The Middle Ages

B The Jurassic period

C The Bronze Age

D The Stone Age

7 **Which of the following is a poem written in the Middle Ages?**

A *The Tyger*

B *Sir Gawain and the Green Knight*

C *Far From the Madding Crowd*

D *Brief Encounter*

8 **During the Middle Ages, parliaments were called when the king needed to consult the nobles and for what other reason?**

A To lower taxes

B To create new lords

C To raise money

D To call elections

9 **Which TWO of the following are 20th-century British discoveries or inventions?**

A The Turing machine

B X-Ray machines

C Magnetic Resonance Imaging (MRI)

D Digital calculators

10   Is the statement below TRUE or FALSE?
The first Union Flag was created in 1606.

A True

B False

11   At the beginning of the 19th century, which one of the following groups could vote?

A All adults over the age of 18

B All women who owned property

C Property-owning men over the age of 21

D Property-owning men over the age of 18

12   Lewis Hamilton is a leading figure in which sport?

A Motor racing

B Horse racing

C Tennis

D Squash

13   Which of the following statements is correct?

A Charles II's son, James, took the throne after he died.

B Charles II had no legitimate children, so his brother James took the throne after he died.

14   Why is William the Conqueror an important English monarch?

A He defeated the Spanish Armada

B He fought Parliament in the English Civil War

C He broke away from the Catholic church in Rome

D He led the last successful foreign invasion of England

15 The Northern Ireland Assembly can make decisions in which TWO of the following areas?

A Agriculture

B Nuclear energy

C Foreign policy

D The environment

16 Which of the following statements is correct?

A Many of the Viking invaders stayed in Britain, in an area known as the Danelaw.

B Many of the Viking invaders stayed in Britain, in an area known as Deptford.

17 Is the statement below TRUE or FALSE?
The Labour Party won a majority at the general election of 7 May 2015.

A True

B False

18 Which of the following are associated with the Iron Age?

A Hill forts

B Giant's Causeway

C The White Tower

D Stained glass windows

19 Which of the following statements is correct?

A You should always introduce yourself to your neighbours when you move into a new house or flat.

B You should never introduce yourself to your new neighbours, but should let them introduce themselves.

20 When did Parliament as we know it today begin to develop?

- **A** The Iron Age
- **B** The Stone Age
- **C** The Middle Ages
- **D** The Bronze Age

21 Which TWO actions can political parties undertake to gain support for their candidate?

- **A** Threatening people to make them vote a certain way
- **B** Handing out leaflets
- **C** Knocking on doors and talking to people about their candidate
- **D** Paying people to vote a certain way

22 In the 19th century the UK became a world centre for which of the following sectors or industries?

- **A** Financial services
- **B** Agriculture
- **C** Wine-making
- **D** Entertainment

23 After the 2010 General Election saw no political party win an overall majority for the first time since 1974, the Conservative Party formed a coalition government with which party?

- **A** Green Party
- **B** Labour Party
- **C** Liberal Democrats
- **D** UKIP

24 Which of the following is the role of a PCSO?

- **A** Representing clients in court
- **B** Supporting police officers at crime scenes and major events
- **C** Deciding a verdict in court
- **D** Treating injured people

ANSWERS: PRACTICE TEST 11

#			Study material reference
1	D	Scotland	p130–3
2	C	National parks	p94
3	A	True	p13
4	A	A fleet of Spanish ships	p24–5
5	A	True	p90–1
6	D	The Stone Age	p12–3
7	B	*Sir Gawain and the Green Knight*	p86–8
8	C	To raise money	p18–9
9	A	The Turing machine	p56–7
	C	Magnetic Resonance Imaging (MRI)	
10	A	True	p40
11	C	Property-owning men over the age of 21	p106
12	A	Motor racing	p78
13	B	Charles II had no legitimate children, so his brother James took the throne after he died.	p31
14	D	He led the last successful foreign invasion of England	p15–6
15	A	Agriculture	p115–9
	D	The environment	
16	A	Many of the Viking invaders stayed in Britain, in an area known as the Danelaw.	p15
17	B	False	p60
18	A	Hill forts	p12–3
19	A	You should always introduce yourself to your neighbours when you move into a new house or flat.	p141
20	C	The Middle Ages	p18–9
21	B	Handing out leaflets	p143
	C	Knocking on doors and talking to people about their candidate	
22	A	Financial services	p41–2
23	C	Liberal Democrats	p60
24	B	Supporting police officers at crime scenes and major events	p127–8

PRACTICE TEST 12

1   **Is the statement below TRUE or FALSE?**
The Bayeux Tapestry commemorates a military victory for William the Conqueror.

   A True

   B False

2   **Is the statement below TRUE or FALSE?**
Eid ul Adha and Eid al-Fitr are religious festivals celebrated by Muslims in the UK.

   A True

   B False

3   **Charles I believed in, and tried to rule in line with, what principle?**

   A Democracy

   B Communism

   C Religious virtue

   D The Divine Right of Kings

4   **Who is the current heir to the throne?**

   A Prince Philip

   B Prince Charles

   C The Prime Minister

   D Prince Harry

5   The UK belongs to which TWO international bodies?

   A The Commonwealth

   B Collective Security Treaty Organization (CSTO)

   C The North Atlantic Free Trade Agreement (NAFTA)

   D The North Atlantic Treaty Organization (NATO)

6   During the First World War the British fought against countries including Germany, the Ottoman Empire and the Austro-Hungarian Empire. What was this alliance known as?

   A The Middle Powers

   B The Central Powers

   C The Germanic Powers

   D The Autocratic Powers

7   Is the statement below TRUE or FALSE?
Breaking a Forced Marriage Protection Order can result in a prison sentence.

   A True

   B False

8   Which composer, born in 1874, wrote *The Planets*?

   A Gustav Holst

   B Ralph Vaughan Williams

   C Sir Edward Elgar

   D Benjamin Britten

9   Which of the following Stone Age monuments is a World Heritage Site found in Wiltshire?

   A Stonehenge

   B Skara Brae

   C The White Tower

   D Sutton Hoo

10 Which of these is a major outdoor music festival?

- **A** Monty Python's Flying Circus
- **B** Isle of Wight Festival
- **C** The Great Exhibition
- **D** The Grand National

11 Who could not get Parliament to agree to their religious and foreign policy views and tried to rule without Parliament?

- **A** Charles I
- **B** Elizabeth I
- **C** Bloody Mary
- **D** Henry VIII

12 Is the statement below TRUE or FALSE?
In the UK it is acceptable to discriminate against people because of their religious beliefs.

- **A** True
- **B** False

13 During the reign of which king was the Domesday Book compiled?

- **A** Harold
- **B** William the Conqueror
- **C** Kenneth MacAlpin
- **D** Alfred the Great

14 Which TWO of the following deal with civil disputes?

- **A** Sheriff Court
- **B** Crown Court
- **C** County Court
- **D** Youth Court

15 Which of the following is a core value of the civil service?

- **A** Laziness
- **B** Party loyalty
- **C** Integrity
- **D** Bribery

16 How often must a car over three years old have an MOT test?

- **A** Every six months
- **B** Every year
- **C** Every three years
- **D** Never

17 Is the statement below TRUE or FALSE?
King Henry I was on the throne at the time of the Magna Carta.

- **A** True
- **B** False

18 Which king united the people of modern-day Scotland to protect them from the threat of Viking attacks?

- **A** Kenneth MacAlpin
- **B** Robert Bruce
- **C** Robert Burns
- **D** William Wallace

19 In which country are Loch Lomond and the Trossachs National Park found?

- **A** Wales
- **B** England
- **C** Scotland
- **D** Northern Ireland

20 A poll card includes which TWO pieces of information?

- **A** The date of the election
- **B** Who you should vote for
- **C** Where the polling station or polling place is located
- **D** How much tax you should pay

21 Who was William Shakespeare?

- **A** A naval commander
- **B** A Scottish patriot
- **C** An English parliamentarian
- **D** A poet, actor and playwright

22 A delay in introducing Home Rule to Ireland resulted in the Easter Rising, which took place in which city?

- **A** Belfast
- **B** Dublin
- **C** Cork
- **D** London

23 Is the statement below TRUE or FALSE?
Everyone pays the correct amount of income tax through PAYE.

- **A** True
- **B** False

24 Is the statement below TRUE or FALSE?
Equal treatment under law means that the law applies in the same way to everyone, as long as they were born in the UK.

- **A** True
- **B** False

ANSWERS: PRACTICE TEST 12

			Study material reference
1	A	True	p15–6
2	A	True	p70–1
3	D	The Divine Right of Kings	p27–8
4	B	Prince Charles	p107–9
5	A	The Commonwealth	p123–5
	D	The North Atlantic Treaty Organization (NATO)	
6	B	The Central Powers	p46–7
7	A	True	p137
8	A	Gustav Holst	p79–81
9	A	Stonehenge	p12–3
10	B	Isle of Wight Festival	p79–81
11	A	Charles I	p27–8
12	B	False	p136
13	B	William the Conqueror	p15–6
14	A	Sheriff Court	p130–3
	C	County Court	
15	C	Integrity	p115
16	B	Every year	p139
17	B	False	p18–9
18	A	Kenneth MacAlpin	p15
19	C	Scotland	p95–103
20	A	The date of the election	p121
	C	Where the polling station or polling place is located	
21	D	A poet, actor and playwright	p26
22	B	Dublin	p47–8
23	B	False	p137–8
24	B	False	p126–7

PRACTICE TEST 13

1   Which of the following statements is correct?

A Trading hours for shops in the UK do not change on public holidays.

B Trading hours for shops in the UK are generally reduced on public holidays.

2   Is the statement below TRUE or FALSE?
Juries are responsible for interpreting the law and ensuring that trials are conducted fairly.

A True

B False

3   Mary Stuart, the queen of Scotland, was often known by which other name?

A Mary Tudor

B Bloody Mary

C Mary, Queen of the Highlands

D Mary, Queen of Scots

4   Which famous composer was born in 1857 in Worcester, England and wrote the *Pomp and Circumstance Marches*?

A Sir William Walton

B George Frederick Handel

C Henry Purcell

D Sir Edward Elgar

5   Which of the following statements is correct?

A Roald Dahl served in the Royal Air Force during the Second World War.

B Roald Dahl served in the Royal Navy during the Second World War.

6   Is the statement below TRUE or FALSE?
Winston Churchill became Britain's Prime Minister
in the early years of the Second World War.

A True

B False

7   In which TWO places are arrangements different
for taking the Life in the UK Test?

A Scotland

B Northern Ireland

C Isle of Man

D Channel Islands

8   Who of the following was a co-discoverer of insulin?

A John Logie Baird

B Sir Frank Whittle

C John MacLeod

D Sir Robert Watson-Watt

9   The first day of one notorious battle in 1916 resulted in
60,000 British casualties. What was this battle?

A The Battle of the Somme

B The Battle of the Bulge

C The Battle of Agincourt

D The Battle of the River Plate

10   Which of the following is a principle guarded by the
European Convention on Human Rights?

A The prohibition of slavery and forced labour

B Free movement globally

C The right to happiness

D The right to bear arms

11 During which king's reign in 1665 was there a major outbreak of plague in London?

- **A** Charles II
- **B** James I
- **C** James II
- **D** Charles I

12 What were women campaigning for the right to vote known as?

- **A** Suffragettes
- **B** Votettes
- **C** Democrettes
- **D** Feminettes

13 Is the statement below TRUE or FALSE?
Through the Middle Ages, English and Scottish law developed in exactly the same way.

- **A** True
- **B** False

14 Is the statement below TRUE or FALSE?
Charles I was interested in science and during his reign, the Royal Society was formed.

- **A** True
- **B** False

15 Which TWO of these careers did Winston Churchill follow before becoming a Conservative MP in 1900?

- **A** Teacher
- **B** Vicar
- **C** Journalist
- **D** Soldier

16 What did missionaries teach the Anglo-Saxons?

- **A** About other cultures
- **B** About Christianity
- **C** About other languages
- **D** About trade

17 Is the statement below TRUE or FALSE?
The Houses of Lancaster and York used red and white roses as their respective symbols.

- **A** True
- **B** False

18 Is the statement below TRUE or FALSE?
The famous books Treasure Island *and* Dr Jekyll and Mr Hyde *were written by Kingsley Amis.*

- **A** True
- **B** False

19 Who wrote *Paradise Lost*?

- **A** William Shakespeare
- **B** Salman Rushdie
- **C** Rider Haggard
- **D** John Milton

20 The Festival of Lights is another name for which of the following?

- **A** Vaisakhi
- **B** Christmas
- **C** Diwali
- **D** Eid ul Adha

21 Anyone who wishes to stand for public office must be at least what age?

- **A** 16
- **B** 18
- **C** 21
- **D** 25

22 The game of golf is traditionally thought to have originated in which country?

- **A** England
- **B** Spain
- **C** USA
- **D** Scotland

23 Is the statement below TRUE or FALSE?
The Good Friday Agreement is also known as the Belfast Agreement.

- **A** True
- **B** False

24 Which TWO of the following are British inventions?

- **A** Jet engine
- **B** Helicopter
- **C** Golf cart
- **D** Hovercraft

ANSWERS: PRACTICE TEST 13

			Study material reference
1	B	Trading hours for shops in the UK are generally reduced on public holidays.	p89
2	B	False	p129–30
3	D	Mary, Queen of Scots	p25
4	D	Sir Edward Elgar	p79–81
5	A	Roald Dahl served in the Royal Air Force during the Second World War.	p59
6	A	True	p48–52
7	C	Isle of Man	p4
	D	Channel Islands	
8	C	John MacLeod	p56–7
9	A	The Battle of the Somme	p46–7
10	A	The prohibition of slavery and forced labour	p135–6
11	A	Charles II	p30–1
12	A	Suffragettes	p43–4
13	B	False	p18–9
14	B	False	p30–1
15	C	Journalist	p50
	D	Soldier	
16	B	About Christianity	p13–5
17	A	True	p21
18	B	False	p85–6
19	D	John Milton	p86–8
20	C	Diwali	p70–1
21	B	18	p121–2
22	D	Scotland	p77
23	A	True	p115–9
24	A	Jet engine	p56–7
	D	Hovercraft	

PRACTICE TEST 14

1   Which of the following is a benefit of volunteering?

   A Getting more state benefits

   B Getting paid

   C Having a chance to practise your English

   D A courtesy car

2   What did hereditary peers lose in 1999?

   A The right to own land

   B The automatic right to sit in the House of Lords

   C The right to elect other peers to the House of Lords

   D The right to speak in Parliament

3   Jane Seymour gave birth to the son Henry VIII wanted. What was his name?

   A Henry

   B Edmund

   C Edward

   D Richard

4   If you can't make it to a polling station to vote you can register for which of the following?

   A A postal ballot

   B An absentee ballot

   C A public ballot

   D A virtual ballot

5 **Is the following statement TRUE or FALSE?**
The Elizabethan period is remembered for the richness of its poetry and drama, especially the plays and poems of William Shakespeare.

A True

B False

6 **Is this statement TRUE or FALSE?**
During Queen Victoria's reign the French Empire became the largest empire the world has ever seen.

A True

B False

7 **Who decides what should happen in legal disputes over contracts, property rights or employment rights?**

A The media

B The police

C The judiciary

D The peers

8 **During the 18th century, Britain fought a number of wars with which country?**

A India

B South Africa

C Scotland

D France

9 **Which of the following statements is correct?**

A The National Assembly for Wales and the Welsh government are based in Edinburgh.

B The National Assembly for Wales and the Welsh government are based in Cardiff.

10 Which of the following statements is correct?

A The Commonwealth is a group of countries which support each other and work together.

B The Commonwealth is a group of regions which compete together at the Olympics.

11 Is the statement below TRUE or FALSE?
Sir Mo Farah was the first person to sail around the world single-handed.

A True

B False

12 What was depicted in the stained glass windows of many cathedrals built in the Middle Ages?

A Stories about kings and coronations

B Stories about battles and victories

C Stories about the Bible and saints

D Stories about communities and farming

13 Is the statement below TRUE or FALSE?
St Columba became the first Archbishop of Canterbury.

A True

B False

14 Which TWO things is Sake Dean Mahomet most famous for?

A Opening the first curry house in Britain

B Resisting British colonialism in Bengal

C He was a general in the Bengal army

D Introducing shampooing (Indian head massage) to Britain

15 Which of the following statements is correct?

A Members of the House of Lords can stand for public office but not for election to the House of Commons.

B Members of the House of Lords can stand for election to any public office.

16 Which organisation was founded in 1895 and now has over 61,000 volunteers helping to preserve important buildings, the countryside and the coastline?

A The National Trust

B The Countryside Alliance

C Country Landowners Association

D The National Gardens Scheme

17 Which of the following was the composer Ralph Vaughan Williams strongly influenced by?

A German folk music

B Scottish folk music

C English folk music

D Irish folk music

18 During the reign of Henry VII what happened to the power of the nobility in England?

A It was reduced

B It increased

C It was abolished

D It was absolute

19 Which of these is a famous UK landmark?

A Loch Lomond and the Trossachs National Park

B Yellowstone Park

C The Brandenburg Gate

D The Black Forest

20 **During the 19th century, Britain and the East India Company gained control of large parts of which TWO countries?**

    A The United States

    B Canada

    C India

    D Singapore

21 **Is the statement below TRUE or FALSE?**
The Hundred Years War between England and France lasted 99 years.

    A True

    B False

22 **What did the Act of Union create?**

    A An official body to protect the rights of workers

    B The joint rule of William and Mary

    C The balance of power between the monarchy and Parliament

    D The Kingdom of Great Britain

23 **Which TWO of the following former colonies were granted independence in 1947?**

    A Pakistan

    B Sierra Leone

    C Jamaica

    D Ceylon (now Sri Lanka)

24 **Which famous religious building has been the coronation church since 1066 and is the final resting place for 17 monarchs?**

    A Westminster Abbey

    B York Minster

    C St Paul's Cathedral

    D Westminster Cathedral

ANSWERS: PRACTICE TEST 14

			Study material reference
1	C	Having a chance to practise your English	p144–6
2	B	The automatic right to sit in the House of Lords	p111
3	C	Edward	p22–4
4	A	A postal ballot	p121
5	A	True	p25–6
6	B	False	p41
7	C	The judiciary	p129–30
8	D	France	p38–9
9	B	The National Assembly for Wales and the Welsh government are based in Cardiff.	p115–9
10	A	The Commonwealth is a group of countries which support each other and work together.	p123–4
11	B	False	p74–5
12	C	Stories about the Bible and saints	p19–21
13	B	False	p13–5
14	A	Opening the first curry house in Britain	p37
	D	Introducing shampooing (Indian head massage) to Britain	
15	A	Members of the House of Lords can stand for public office but not for election to the House of Commons.	p121–2
16	A	The National Trust	p94
17	C	English folk music	p79–81
18	A	It was reduced	p22–4
19	A	Loch Lomond and the Trossachs National Park	p95–103
20	B	Canada	p35–7
	C	India	
21	B	False	p17
22	D	The Kingdom of Great Britain	p34
23	A	Pakistan	p52–4
	D	Ceylon (now Sri Lanka)	
24	A	Westminster Abbey	p68

PRACTICE TEST 15

1   **During the 19th century, which sector of the Irish economy supported around two-thirds of its people?**

   A Tourism

   B Farming

   C Manufacturing

   D Shipbuilding

2   **Which of the following statements is correct?**

   A During the Elizabethan period, English settlers began to colonise America.

   B During the Elizabethan period, English settlers began to colonise Australia.

3   **Which of the following factors contributed to the Industrial Revolution in Britain?**

   A The foundation of the modern welfare state

   B The development of steam power and machinery

   C The outbreak of plague

   D The end of the Second World War

4   **Which of the following statements is correct?**

   A The Beveridge Report of 1942 outlined a plan to end the war in Europe.

   B The Beveridge Report of 1942 provided the basis of the modern welfare state.

5   By 1200, the English ruled an area of Ireland around Dublin known as what?

  A The Light

  B The Pict

  C The Pale

  D The Plain

6   Official reports of parliamentary proceedings are published in which of the following?

  A Juilliard

  B Hansard

  C The Telegraph

  D The Sunday Times

7   Which of these sectors was nationalised by the post-war Labour government?

  A Coal mining

  B The banks

  C The airlines

  D Farming

8   Is this statement TRUE or FALSE?
In Wales the established Church is the Church of Wales.

  A True

  B False

9   Which king invaded Ireland in the seventeenth century in an attempt to regain the throne with an army from France?

  A Henry V

  B James II

  C Kenneth MacAlpin

  D John

10 Which of the following statements is correct?

A   You will need the help of a lawyer to issue a small claim.

B   You do not need the help of a lawyer to issue a small claim.

11 Which of the following introduced new limits to the monarch's powers to raise taxes or administer justice in the seventeenth century?

A   The Declaration of Rights

B   The Butler Act

C   The Good Friday Agreement

D   The Abolition Act

12 Why were castles built in Britain and Ireland in the Middle Ages?

A   They were cheap to build

B   They were defensive strongholds

C   They were status symbols for the nobility

D   They created work for tradesmen

13 Which of the following statements is correct?

A   11 November commemorates soldiers who died in the First World War as well as those who have died in all conflicts involving the UK since then.

B   11 November only commemorates soldiers who died in the First World War.

14 Is the statement below TRUE or FALSE?
The BBC began the world's first regular television service in 1936.

A   True

B   False

15 Which artist is considered to be the one who raised the profile of landscape painting?

   A John Constable

   B Thomas Gainsborough

   C David Allan

   D Joseph Turner

16 How is the British Broadcasting Corporation (BBC) funded?

   A With money raised from television licences

   B Through sponsorship by large national and multinational companies

   C Through advertising revenue

   D By selling subscription services

17 Is the statement below TRUE or FALSE?
The Archbishop of Canterbury opens the new Parliamentary session each year.

   A True

   B False

18 Which of the following is a famous tennis tournament played in the UK every year?

   A Wimbledon

   B The Grand National

   C The Open

   D Six Nations

19 Which of the following statements is correct?

   A Margaret Thatcher was the longest-serving Prime Minister of the UK in the 20th century.

   B Margaret Thatcher was the second longest-serving Prime Minister of the UK in the 20th century.

20 What happened when Charles I tried to impose a revised Prayer Book onto the Presbyterian Church in Scotland?

   A The Scottish rebelled and formed an army

   B It was very popular across the Union

   C It was accepted after some amendments

   D The Pope came to England to help Charles I

21 Can young people in every part of the UK volunteer with the National Citizen Service?

   A Yes, but each part of the UK has a different website for information about the service

   B No, only young people resident in England can volunteer

22 St George is the patron saint of which country?

   A England

   B Scotland

   C Wales

   D Northern Ireland

23 Is the statement below TRUE or FALSE?
The American colonies rebelled against the British Parliament in the 18th century because they didn't want to pay taxes without representation in Parliament.

   A True

   B False

24 Which TWO of the following changes to welfare happened in the 1940s?

   A The National Health Service was founded

   B Women were granted the right to equal pay

   C A national social security system was introduced

   D Workers unions were abolished

ANSWERS: PRACTICE TEST 15

			Study material reference
1	B	Farming	p43
2	A	During the Elizabethan period, English settlers began to colonise America.	p25–6
3	B	The development of steam power and machinery	p35–7
4	B	The Beveridge Report of 1942 provided the basis of the modern welfare state.	p52
5	C	The Pale	p17
6	B	Hansard	p119
7	A	Coal mining	p52
8	B	False	p67
9	B	James II	p31–2
10	B	You do not need the help of a lawyer to issue a small claim.	p133–4
11	A	The Declaration of Rights	p33
12	B	They were defensive strongholds	p19–21
13	A	11 November commemorates soldiers who died in the First World War as well as those who have died in all conflicts involving the UK since then.	p72–3
14	A	True	p48
15	D	Joseph Turner	p82–3
16	A	With money raised from television licences	p92–3
17	B	False	p107–9
18	A	Wimbledon	p78
19	A	Margaret Thatcher was the longest-serving Prime Minister of the UK in the 20th century.	p58
20	A	The Scottish rebelled and formed an army	p28
21	A	Yes, but each part of the UK has a different website for information about the service	p144–6
22	A	England	p67–8
23	A	True	p38
24	A	The National Health Service was founded	p52
	C	A national social security system was introduced	

PRACTICE TEST 16

1 **Some people in Britain were opposed to the slave trade. Who set up the first formal anti-slavery groups in the late 1700s?**

    A Methodists

    B Mormons

    C Quakers

    D Puritans

2 **What is the capital city of Scotland?**

    A Edinburgh

    B Glasgow

    C Dundee

    D Aberdeen

3 **The Elizabethan period in England was a time of growing patriotism. What do we mean by this?**

    A There was unrest and instability

    B The monarchy became unpopular

    C The country became more democratic

    D There was a feeling of pride in being English

4 **On which day do people send cards anonymously to someone they admire?**

    A Christmas Day

    B New Year's Day

    C Valentine's Day

    D April Fool's Day

5 **As well as giving legal advice, solicitors are able to do which TWO of the following?**

   A Represent clients in court

   B Arrest suspects

   C Take action for a client

   D Change the law

6 **Which TWO of the following countries are members of the Commonwealth?**

   A USA

   B Pakistan

   C Canada

   D Brazil

7 **Which of the following was a change demanded by the Chartists?**

   A For elections to be stopped

   B For MPs to be paid

   C Equal voting rights for women

   D For prisoners to have the right to a court hearing

8 **Which of the following is a document or piece of legislation that sets out fundamental rights or freedoms?**

   A The UK Constitution

   B The Habeas Corpus Act

   C The Statute of Rhuddlan

   D The Act of Union

9 **Is the statement below TRUE or FALSE?**
Henry VIII continued his father's work to centralise the administrative powers of England.

   A True

   B False

10 In which part of the UK was pioneering doctor
Alexander Fleming born in 1881?

- **A** Wales
- **B** Scotland
- **C** East Anglia
- **D** Cornwall

11 Which of the following statements is correct?

- **A** At its peak the British Empire had an estimated population of just under 400 million.
- **B** At its peak the British Empire had an estimated population of just under 4 million.

12 In 1913, the British government promised Home Rule for Ireland.
Which group within Ireland threatened to resist this move by force?

- **A** The Protestants in the south
- **B** The Catholics in the north
- **C** The Catholics in the south
- **D** The Protestants in the north

13 Is the statement below TRUE or FALSE?
In 1688, Protestant leaders in England asked William of Orange to invade England and proclaim himself king.

- **A** True
- **B** False

14 Is the statement below TRUE or FALSE?
All MPs represent one of the main political parties.

- **A** True
- **B** False

15 Who were the Picts?

    A Ancestors of the Irish people

    B Ancestors of the Welsh people

    C Ancestors of the Scottish people

    D Ancestors of the English people

16 At which of the following famous UK landmarks would you find biomes?

    A Giant's Causeway

    B The Eden Project

    C Snowdonia

    D Edinburgh Castle

17 During the English Civil War, in which TWO battles was Charles I's army defeated?

    A Battle of Bosworth Field

    B Battle of Naseby

    C Battle of Marston Moor

    D Battle of Hastings

18 Which TWO of the following were wives of Henry VIII?

    A Elizabeth of York

    B Catherine Parr

    C Catherine Raleigh

    D Jane Seymour

19 Is the statement below TRUE or FALSE?
Anyone over the age of 14 can legally buy tobacco products in the UK.

    A True

    B False

20 **Which Northern Irish portrait artist, who died in 1941, painted portraits of the Royal Family?**

- **A** Sir John Lavery
- **B** Paul Henry
- **C** Basil Blackshaw
- **D** Markey Robinson

21 **Is the statement below TRUE or FALSE?**
Charles II was crowned King of England, Wales, Scotland and Ireland in the Restoration after the English Civil War.

- **A** True
- **B** False

22 **Which TWO of the following are Protestant Christian groups?**

- **A** Baptists
- **B** Quakers
- **C** Hare Krishnas
- **D** Roman Catholics

23 **What TWO of the following are roles of a constitutional monarch?**

- **A** To appoint the democratically elected government
- **B** To open the new parliamentary session each year
- **C** To raise new taxes
- **D** To lead the armed forces into battle

24 **Pumpkins, lit with candles, are used to celebrate which traditional festival?**

- **A** Bonfire Night
- **B** Halloween
- **C** Midsummer
- **D** Mayday

ANSWERS: PRACTICE TEST 16

			Study material reference
1	C	Quakers	p37–8
2	A	Edinburgh	p62–3
3	D	There was a feeling of pride in being English	p25–6
4	C	Valentine's Day	p72–3
5	A	Represent clients in court	p134–5
	C	Take action for a client	
6	B	Pakistan	p123–4
	C	Canada	
7	B	For MPs to be paid	p106
8	B	The Habeas Corpus Act	p135–6
9	A	True	p22–4
10	B	Scotland	p52
11	A	At its peak the British Empire had an estimated population of just under 400 million.	p41
12	D	The Protestants in the north	p47–8
13	A	True	p31–2
14	B	False	p114
15	C	Ancestors of the Scottish people	p13
16	B	The Eden Project	p95–103
17	B	Battle of Naseby	p28–30
	C	Battle of Marston Moor	
18	B	Catherine Parr	p23
	D	Jane Seymour	
19	B	False	p126–7
20	A	Sir John Lavery	p82–3
21	A	True	p30–1
22	A	Baptists	p67
	B	Quakers	
23	A	To appoint the democratically elected government	p107–9
	B	To open the parliamentary session each year	
24	B	Halloween	p72–3

PRACTICE TEST 17

1   **Why is William III's accession to the throne known as the Glorious Revolution?**

   A It signalled the start of the Hundred Years War

   B William of Orange defeated a much larger army

   C It led to the Reformation and the formation of the Protestant Church

   D There was no fighting in England

2   **Which of the following statements is correct?**

   A During the reign of Charles I, Parliament attempted to take control of the English army following a rebellion in Ireland.

   B During the reign of Charles I, Irish Catholics supported the views of the Puritans.

3   **Which political party was Clement Attlee a member of?**

   A Liberal Democrats

   B Conservative

   C Green

   D Labour

4   **Britain played a leading role in coalition forces, during the 1990s, in a conflict in which country?**

   A The Maldives

   B The former Republic of Yugoslavia

   C South Africa

   D France

5   Is the statement below TRUE or FALSE?
There are no differences between the court systems of
England, Northern Ireland, Scotland and Wales.

   A True

   B False

6   Which of the following statements is correct?

   A By 1400, in England, official documents were being
       written in English and English was the preferred
       language of Parliament and the royal court.

   B By 1400, a mixture of Norman French and Anglo-Saxon was
       being spoken and no unified language was emerging.

7   George and Robert Stephenson are famous for pioneering what?

   A The railway engine

   B The aeroplane

   C The telephone

   D The electric lightbulb

8   Is the statement below TRUE or FALSE?
At the time of the Reformation, Protestants believed that
a person's own relationship with God was more important
than submitting to the authority of the Church.

   A True

   B False

9   Which of the following statements is correct?

   A Completed ballots must be handed to an election official.

   B Completed ballots must be placed in a ballot box.

10 Is the statement below TRUE or FALSE?
    In the UK, everybody has the right to choose their
    religion or choose not to practise a religion.

    A True

    B False

11 **Which of the following statements is correct?**

    A In Scotland, serious offences are tried in a Sheriff Court.

    B In Scotland, serious offences are tried in a Crown Court.

12 Is the statement below TRUE or FALSE?
    During the Iron Age people spoke languages
    from the Celtic language family.

    A True

    B False

13 **When England became a republic, after Charles I lost**
    the English Civil War, it no longer had what?

    A A parliament

    B A national anthem

    C A monarch

    D A Prime Minister

14 Is the statement below TRUE or FALSE?
    In 1690, following his unsuccessful attempt to regain his
    throne in Ireland, James II fled back to the Netherlands.

    A True

    B False

15 Income tax is paid on which of the following forms of income?

    A Shopping vouchers

    B Money you win on the lottery

    C Pension payments

    D Small gifts of money

16 Which of the following statements is correct?

    A The small claims procedure is an informal way of helping people who have been victims of identity theft or fraud.

    B The small claims procedure is an informal way of helping people settle minor disputes without needing a lawyer.

17 Which of the following is a British invention or innovation?

    A A Turing machine

    B Micro Machines

    C Superglue

    D The photocopier

18 Which of the following statements is correct?

    A The public may not listen to debates in the House of Commons or the House of Lords.

    B The public may listen to debates in the House of Commons and the House of Lords.

19 Is the statement below TRUE or FALSE?
The Houses of Parliament were built in the 19th century when the medieval 'gothic' style of architecture was popular.

    A True

    B False

20 **Which famous UK landmark is home to the Elizabeth Tower and Big Ben?**

   A St Paul's Cathedral

   B Houses of Parliament

   C The Tower of London

   D Buckingham Palace

21 **Is it possible for the leader of the opposition to become Prime Minister?**

   A Yes, if the Prime Minister resigns

   B Yes, if his or her party wins a General Election

22 **People traditionally spend Christmas Day at home and enjoy a special meal that includes which meat?**

   A Duck

   B Turkey

   C Guinea fowl

   D Pork

23 **Is the following statement TRUE or FALSE?**
The UK is a permanent member of the UN Security Council.

   A True

   B False

24 **Which Acts of Parliament, passed in 1832 and 1867, abolished rotten boroughs, gave more parliamentary seats to urban areas and greatly increased the right of people to vote?**

   A The Change Acts

   B The Voting Acts

   C The Election Acts

   D The Reform Acts

ANSWERS: PRACTICE TEST 17

			Study material reference
1	D	There was no fighting in England	p31–2
2	A	During the reign of Charles I, Parliament attempted to take control of the English army following a rebellion in Ireland.	p28
3	D	Labour	p52–4
4	B	The former Republic of Yugoslavia	p59–60
5	B	False	p130–3
6	A	By 1400, in England, official documents were being written in English and English was the preferred language of Parliament and the royal court.	p19–21
7	A	The railway engine	p41–2
8	A	True	p22–4
9	B	Completed ballots must be placed in a ballot box.	p121
10	A	True	p66–7
11	A	In Scotland, serious offences are tried in a Sheriff Court.	p130–3
12	A	True	p12–3
13	C	A monarch	p28–30
14	B	False	p31–2
15	C	Pension payments	p137–8
16	B	The small claims procedure is an informal way of helping people settle minor disputes without needing a lawyer.	p133–4
17	A	A Turing machine	p56–7
18	B	The public may listen to debates in the House of Commons and the House of Lords.	p122–3
19	A	True	p84–5
20	B	Houses of Parliament	p95–103
21	B	Yes, if his or her party wins a General Election	p114
22	B	Turkey	p69–70
23	A	True	p125
24	D	The Reform Acts	p43–4

PRACTICE TEST 18

1 **Police forces are headed by whom?**

- **A** Ministers
- **B** Generals
- **C** Mayors
- **D** Chief Constables

2 **Is the statement below TRUE or FALSE?**
A Formula 1 Grand Prix race is held in Britain every year.

- **A** True
- **B** False

3 **Which of the following statements is correct?**

- **A** There are only a few charities in Britain, most of them national.
- **B** There are thousands of charities active in Britain.

4 **During the 1960s, Parliament passed new laws that gave women which right?**

- **A** Free lunches
- **B** Equal pay
- **C** Childcare at work
- **D** Two years' paid maternity leave

5 **Who wrote the piece of music *Belshazzar's Feast*?**

- **A** Henry Purcell
- **B** Sir William Walton
- **C** Gustav Holst
- **D** Sir Edward Elgar

6   Is the statement below TRUE or FALSE?
The 1970s was a time of serious unrest in Northern Ireland.

   A True

   B False

7   The UK joined which international organisation in 1973?

   A The UN

   B NATO

   C The Commonwealth

   D The EEC

8   How were Elizabeth I and Mary, Queen of Scots related?

   A They were sisters

   B They were cousins

   C Mary was Elizabeth's daughter

   D They were half-sisters

9   Which of these countries fought on the side of the Allied Powers during the First World War?

   A Bulgaria

   B Italy

   C Germany

   D Chile

10   King Edward I of England annexed Wales to the crown of England by which statute?

   A The Statute of Caernarfon

   B The Statute of Gwynedd

   C The Statute of Carmarthen

   D The Statute of Rhuddlan

11 Where in London is the White Tower?

- **A** Tower of London
- **B** Buckingham Palace
- **C** Palace of Westminster
- **D** St Paul's Cathedral

12 Is the statement below TRUE or FALSE?
The Reformation failed in Scotland and the country remained strongly Catholic.

- **A** True
- **B** False

13 Who was Henry VIII's first wife?

- **A** Elizabeth of York
- **B** Catherine Howard
- **C** Catherine of Aragon
- **D** Mary, Queen of Scots

14 Who won the English Civil War in 1646?

- **A** Parliament
- **B** The Cavaliers
- **C** The Jacobites
- **D** The House of York

15 What special type of windows did many cathedrals built in the Middle Ages have?

- **A** Arched
- **B** Mullioned
- **C** Stained glass
- **D** Sash

16 Which of the following statements is correct?

- **A** Countries must join the Commonwealth if the monarch commands it.
- **B** Countries join the Commonwealth voluntarily.

17 Which TWO of the following names may be given to the day before Lent starts?

- **A** Ash Wednesday
- **B** Shrove Tuesday
- **C** Good Friday
- **D** Pancake Day

18 Why is Dame Jessica Ennis-Hill famous?

- **A** She is a successful comedienne
- **B** She writes poetry
- **C** She invented the cash-dispensing ATM
- **D** She is an Olympic gold medallist

19 Which English king led his army to victory at the Battle of Agincourt?

- **A** Henry V
- **B** Henry VII
- **C** Henry II
- **D** Henry VIII

20 During the 17th century, many people left Britain and Ireland to settle in which of the following places?

- **A** France
- **B** Africa
- **C** America
- **D** Germany

21 Is the statement below TRUE or FALSE?
It is legal to carry a weapon if it is for self-defence.

   A True

   B False

22 Which TWO of these were very popular sixties British pop groups?

   A ABBA

   B The Beatles

   C The Rolling Stones

   D The Beach Boys

23 Is the statement below TRUE or FALSE?
Income tax pays for services such as education,
roads and the armed services.

   A True

   B False

24 Fighting broke out between British forces and which
of the following in the late 18th century?

   A Dutch settlers in South Africa

   B The Middle Powers

   C North American colonists

   D The Spanish Armada

ANSWERS: PRACTICE TEST 18

			Study material reference
1	D	Chief Constables	p127–8
2	A	True	p78
3	B	There are thousands of charities active in Britain.	p144–6
4	B	Equal pay	p55
5	B	Sir William Walton	p79–81
6	A	True	p57
7	D	The EEC	p124–5
8	B	They were cousins	p25
9	B	Italy	p46–7
10	D	The Statute of Rhuddlan	p17
11	A	Tower of London	p84–5
12	B	False	p25
13	C	Catherine of Aragon	p23
14	A	Parliament	p28–30
15	C	Stained glass	p19–21
16	B	Countries join the Commonwealth voluntarily.	p123–4
17	B	Shrove Tuesday	p69–70
	D	Pancake Day	
18	D	She is an Olympic gold medallist	p74–5
19	A	Henry V	p17
20	C	America	p34
21	B	False	p126–7
22	B	The Beatles	p55
	C	The Rolling Stones	
23	A	True	p137–8
24	C	North American colonists	p38

PRACTICE TEST 19

1   Who was Cnut, also called Canute?

   A A Danish king of England

   B An Anglo-Saxon king of England

   C A Scottish lord

   D A Viking warrior

2   Which of the following is a ministerial position appointed to the cabinet?

   A The Chancellor of the Exchequer

   B The Speaker

   C The leader of the opposition

   D Chief Constable

3   The Scottish Parliament was originally made up of the lords, the commons, and which of the following?

   A The clergy

   B The Estates

   C The Houses

   D The bishops

4   Is the statement below TRUE or FALSE?
English laws and the English language were introduced to Wales during the Middle Ages.

   A True

   B False

5   Is the statement below TRUE or FALSE?
The Council of Europe is another name for the European Union.

   A True

   B False

6   Which of the following statements is correct?

    A Hugh Hudson is a famous film director who made *Chariots of Fire.*

    B Hugh Hudson is a famous author who wrote *Brighton Rock* and *The Heart of the Matter.*

7   Looking after the environment involves which TWO of the following?

    A Buying new products whenever possible

    B Buying recycled products whenever possible

    C Recycling waste whenever possible

    D Using more energy whenever possible

8   Which of the following statements is correct?

    A If they are married, both parents are equally responsible for their children.

    B If they are married, the woman has sole legal responsibility for a couple's children.

9   Which of the following statements is correct?

    A The Scottish Parliament can pass laws for Scotland on all matters.

    B The Scottish Parliament can only pass legislation for Scotland on certain matters.

10 Who were the Jutes, Angles and Saxons?

    A Tribespeople from northern Europe

    B Romans

    C Tribespeople from Wales

    D Tribespeople from Scotland

11 **Which country's coastline did James Cook map, leading to the establishment of colonies there?**

A Indonesia

B Portugal

C South Africa

D Australia

12 **About which conflict did poets Wilfred Owen and Siegfried Sassoon write?**

A Crimean War

B Boer War

C First World War

D Second World War

13 **Which Jewish religious festival happens in November or December every year?**

A Eid al-Fitr

B Eid ul Adha

C Hannukah

D Vaisakhi

14 **The 'Ashes' are played for between England and Australia in which sport?**

A Rugby union

B Tennis

C Darts

D Cricket

15 **Which of the following statements is correct?**

A Mary, Queen of Scots hoped Elizabeth I might help her regain her throne.

B Mary, Queen of Scots had no faith that Elizabeth I might help her regain her throne.

16 How are people chosen for a jury?

A Randomly, from the electoral register

B Randomly, from the lottery

C People apply to be on a jury

D They are appointed by legal professionals

17 Cowes on the Isle of Wight is famous for which of the following sports?

A Rowing

B Sailing

C Fishing championships

D Surfing

18 What does an MOT test stand for?

A Ministry of Truth test

B Mode of Transport test

C Music and Technology test

D Ministry of Transport test

19 Is the statement below TRUE or FALSE?
Employees need to pay National Insurance Contributions themselves.

A True

B False

20 Which of these is a famous British artist?

A Dame Zaha Hadid

B Sir Edwin Lutyens

C Percy Shelley

D Lucian Freud

21 **Which of James II's relatives were strictly Protestant?**

 A Brothers

B Sisters

C Daughters

D Aunts and uncles

22 **The flag of which nation of the UK has a dragon on it?**

A Scotland

B England

C Wales

D Northern Ireland

23 **Pressure and lobby groups represent the interests of which TWO of the following?**

A Minor political parties

B Foreign ambassadors

C Business organisations

D Campaigning organisations

24 **Is the following statement TRUE or FALSE?**
The title of the UK national anthem is 'Long Live the Queen'.

A True

B False

ANSWERS: PRACTICE TEST 19

#			Study material reference
1	A	A Danish king of England	p15
2	A	The Chancellor of the Exchequer	p113–4
3	A	The clergy	p18–9
4	A	True	p17
5	B	False	p125
6	A	Hugh Hudson is a famous film director who made *Chariots of Fire*.	p90–1
7	B	Buying recycled products whenever possible	p146
	C	Recycling waste whenever possible	
8	A	If they are married, both parents are equally responsible for their children.	p65–6
9	B	The Scottish Parliament can only pass legislation for Scotland on certain matters.	p115–9
10	A	Tribespeople from northern Europe	p13–5
11	D	Australia	p35–7
12	C	First World War	p86–8
13	C	Hannukah	p70–1
14	D	Cricket	p76
15	A	Mary, Queen of Scots hoped Elizabeth I might help her regain her throne.	p25
16	A	Randomly, from the electoral register	p130–3
17	B	Sailing	p78
18	D	Ministry of Transport test	p139
19	B	False	p138–9
20	D	Lucian Freud	p82–3
21	C	Daughters	p31
22	C	Wales	p40
23	C	Business organisations	p114
	D	Campaigning organisations	
24	B	False	p109

PRACTICE TEST 20

1   Is the statement below TRUE or FALSE?
The Scottish Exhibition and Conference Centre is in Edinburgh.

- **A** True
- **B** False

2   Which TWO of the following are famous plays by William Shakespeare?

- **A** *The Duchess of Malfi*
- **B** *Romeo and Juliet*
- **C** *A Midsummer Night's Dream*
- **D** *Dr Faustus*

3   In which British city is the Royal Crescent?

- **A** Bath
- **B** Exeter
- **C** Edinburgh
- **D** Cardiff

4   During which period of the Christian calendar is it traditional to fast?

- **A** Easter
- **B** Christmas
- **C** Lent
- **D** Advent

5   By the middle of the 15th century, what had happened to the last of the Welsh rebellions?

   A They had been defeated by the English

   B They had been contained within Wales

   C They were victorious over the English armies

   D They were abandoned because they were too expensive

6   Which British Admiral was killed at the Battle of Trafalgar?

   A Napoleon

   B Nelson

   C Sir Francis Drake

   D Duke of Wellington

7   Which of the following statements is correct?

   A Civil law relates to crimes which are investigated by the police.

   B Civil law relates to disputes between people.

8   Who was responsible for building the Tower of London?

   A William the Conqueror

   B Edward I

   C Henry VIII

   D Elizabeth I

9   Who was the first Briton to win the Tour de France?

   A Sir Chris Hoy

   B Sir Bradley Wiggins

   C Mark Cavendish

   D Reg Harris

10   Which of the following statements is correct?

   A It is legal to send a girl abroad for circumcision or cutting.

   B It is illegal in the UK to send a girl abroad for circumcision or cutting.

11   Is the statement below TRUE or FALSE?
The Council of Europe has the power to make laws which are binding in member states.

　　A　True

　　B　False

12   Is the statement below TRUE or FALSE?
The famous writer and poet Dylan Thomas was from Scotland.

　　A　True

　　B　False

13   Halloween is regarded historically as which of the following?

　　A　A Christian festival

　　B　A Muslim festival

　　C　A pagan festival

　　D　A Sikh festival

14   Where in Ireland did the English government encourage Scottish and English Protestants to settle during the reigns of Elizabeth I and James I?

　　A　Ulster

　　B　Dublin

　　C　Cork

　　D　Armagh

15   A famous boat race for rowers is contested on the River Thames each year between which university teams?

　　A　Cambridge and London

　　B　Edinburgh and Oxford

　　C　Edinburgh and London

　　D　Cambridge and Oxford

16 **Penicillin was developed into a usable drug by Howard Florey and which other scientist?**

- **A** Stephen Hawking
- **B** Marie Curie
- **C** Albert Einstein
- **D** Ernst Chain

17 **Which artist, born in 1937, is famous for his contribution to the 'pop art' movement of the 1960s?**

- **A** Lucian Freud
- **B** John Petts
- **C** David Hockney
- **D** Robert Lenkiewicz

18 **What does the Victoria Cross, first awarded during the Crimean War, honour?**

- **A** Exceptional journalism by war reporters
- **B** Life-saving care administered by doctors and nurses
- **C** Acts of valour by soldiers
- **D** Outstanding painting skills by war artists

19 **Which of these is a modern UK regional language?**

- **A** Celtic
- **B** Northern
- **C** Gaelic
- **D** Kentish

20 **Which of the statements below is correct?**

- **A** More women than men study at university.
- **B** There are now more female MPs than male MPs.

21 Is the statement below TRUE or FALSE?
Ellie Simmonds is a Paralympian and was the youngest member of the British team at the 2008 games.

   A True

   B False

22 During which decade of the 20th century did the Punk movement happen in Britain?

   A 1950s

   B 1960s

   C 1970s

   D 1980s

23 What kind of Church is the Church of Scotland?

   A Mormon

   B Scientologist

   C Presbyterian

   D Amish

24 Emmeline Pankhurst, who was born in Manchester in 1858, had a role in establishing which TWO organisations for women's rights?

   A The Women's Voting Council

   B The Women's Franchise League

   C The Female Democratic Organisation

   D The Women's Social and Political Union

ANSWERS: PRACTICE TEST 20

			Study material reference
1	B	False	p79–81
2	B	*Romeo and Juliet*	p25–6
	C	*A Midsummer Night's Dream*	
3	A	Bath	p84–5
4	C	Lent	p69–70
5	A	They had been defeated by the English	p17
6	B	Nelson	p38–9
7	B	Civil law relates to disputes between people.	p126–7
8	A	William the Conqueror	p95–103
9	B	Sir Bradley Wiggins	p74–5
10	B	It is illegal in the UK to send a girl abroad for circumcision or cutting.	p137
11	B	False	p125
12	B	False	p54
13	C	A pagan festival	p72–3
14	A	Ulster	p27
15	D	Cambridge and Oxford	p78
16	D	Ernst Chain	p52
17	C	David Hockney	p82–3
18	C	Acts of valour by soldiers	p42–3
19	C	Gaelic	p64
20	A	More women than men study at university.	p65–6
21	A	True	p74–5
22	C	1970s	p79–81
23	C	Presbyterian	p67
24	B	The Women's Franchise League	p44
	D	The Women's Social and Political Union	

You've just taken 20 full tests.

**Best of luck for your official
Life in the UK test.**

Let us know how it goes at
www.lifeintheuk.net/feedback

We'd love to hear your
experiences, good or bad, or any
suggestions you have to help us
make our products better.

GET THE LIFE IN THE UK TEST APP

Take practice tests wherever you go with hundreds of questions and randomised practice tests in your hand.

The essential revision aid for anyone on the move. Find out more at **www.lifeintheuk.net/app**